STORIES FROM LATIN AMERICA

AN ESL/EFL READER

Larry T. Myers

Colegio Universitario de Humacao

Illustrations by
Agnes Pou Rivera

Prentice Hall Regents, Englewood Cliffs, NJ 07632

Library of Congress Cataloging-in-Publication Data

Myers, Larry T., (Date)
　Stories from Latin America.

　1. English language—Text-books for foreign
speakers—Spanish. 2. Readers—Latin America.
3. College readers. 4. Latin America—Fiction.
I. Title.
PE1129.S8M94　1987　　　428.6'461　　　86-25186
ISBN 0-13-850223-4

> To my mother, Mildred,
> my wife, Enilda,
> and my daughters, Inianid and Linda

Editorial/production supervision and interior design:
　Ann L. Mohan, WordCrafters Editorial Services, Inc.

Cover design: Diane Saxe

Manufacturing buyer: Carol Bystrom

© 1987 by Prentice-Hall, Inc.
A Division of Simon & Schuster
Englewood Cliffs, New Jersey 07632

All rights reserved. No part of this book may be
reproduced, in any form or by any means,
without permission in writing from the publisher.

Printed in the United States of America

20　19　18　17　16　15　14　13　12

ISBN　0-13-850223-4　01

Prentice-Hall International (UK) Limited, *London*
Prentice-Hall of Australia Pty. Limited, *Sydney*
Prentice-Hall Canada, Inc., *Toronto*
Prentice-Hall Hispanoamericana, S.A., *Mexico*
Prentice-Hall of India Private Limited, *New Delhi*
Prentice-Hall of Japan, Inc., *Tokyo*
Prentice-Hall of Southeast Asia Pte. Ltd., *Singapore*
Editora Prentice-Hall do Brasil, Ltda., *Rio de Janeiro*

CONTENTS

PREFACE vii

CHAPTER 1
APPEARANCES CAN BE DECEPTIVE 1

Beginning: 660 words
Ending: 110 words

CHAPTER 2
MISS MARIA 7

Beginning: 655 words
Ending: 215 words

CHAPTER 3
THE GENERATION GAP 13

Beginning: 765 words
Ending: 230 words

CHAPTER 4
CARMEN'S TWO BOYFRIENDS 19
Beginning: 435 words
Ending: 260 words

CHAPTER 5
THE MISTAKE 24
Beginning: 1055 words
Ending: 115 words

CHAPTER 6
MEXICO IS BEAUTIFUL 30
Beginning: 290 words
Ending: 255 words

CHAPTER 7
THE TV FRIEND 35
Beginning: 640 words
Ending: 95 words

CHAPTER 8
THE FATAL FRIENDSHIP 41
Beginning: 800 words
Ending: 180 words

CHAPTER 9
THE VIDEO GAME GENIUS 47
Beginning: 305 words
Ending: 180 words

CHAPTER 10
THE LONE SCUBA DIVER 52
Beginning: 695 words
Ending: 240 words

CHAPTER 11
WORKING TO LIVE 58

Beginning: 600 words
Ending: 340 words

CHAPTER 12
THE COSTLY DECISION 64

Beginning: 370 words
Ending: 130 words

CHAPTER 13
THE GOOD SAMARITANS 69

Beginning: 360 words
Ending: 500 words

CHAPTER 14
THE HABIT 75

Beginning: 515 words
Ending: 40 words

CHAPTER 15
THE UGLY SUITOR 80

Beginning: 340 words
Ending: 260 words

CHAPTER 16
SARA 85

Beginning: 1030 words
Ending: 155 words

CHAPTER 17
THE DEATH OF THE MANGO TREE 91

640 words

CHAPTER 18
VICTORY IN THE WATER 97

835 words

CHAPTER 19
THE HANDSOME UGLY BOY   103
590 words

CHAPTER 20
THE ABORTION   109
800 words

CHAPTER 21
THE CHASE   114
470 words

CHAPTER 22
THE OUTSIDER   119
630 words

CHAPTER 23
THE BLIND BASKETBALL PLAYER   124
1850 words

Note: Each story is accompanied by an illustration, prereading, reading guide questions, comprehension questions, questions for further discussion or writing, an optional writing exercise, obtaining meaning from context, and a prediction or cloze exercise.

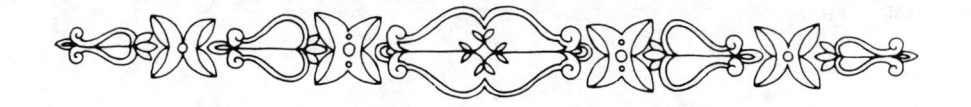

PREFACE

Stories from Latin America is set in Latin America, peopled by Latin Americans, and based on themes and situations derived from discussions with students and firsthand experience. Even the language of the stories includes cognates and other words likely to be familiar to Spanish-speaking people. In addition, revisions of stories and exercises were based on suggestions from students and personnel at Humacao University College and people from all over Latin America.

Level

The book has been used successfully within the public university system of Puerto Rico at the pre-basic, basic, and intermediate levels. It seems best suited to the basic level within this system but might be used at higher or lower levels at other institutions and in other places, depending on the prevalence of English, institutional definitions of levels, and variation from group to group (some basic groups are more advanced than others).

Goal

The main goal of this book is to develop reading fluency. Fluent reading is continuous, relatively fast reading with good comprehension. Studies reveal that the best readers grasp meaning quickly from relatively small samplings of text following a repetitive pattern of sampling, forming hypotheses, and resampling to check their hypotheses.[1] In other words, they read a little and guess the rest. Because they grasp meaning from a small sampling, they read fast. In contrast, poor readers take relatively large samplings and so read slowly. Two of the most common strategies of ESL and EFL students—word-by-word reading and translation (English-Spanish dictionary dependence)—are examples of this. James Coady suggests these strategies are the result of teacher and textbook reinforcement of reading for perfect comprehension.[2] In other words, because reading is treated analytically and detailed comprehension is expected, students feel they must be sure of every word's meaning, and this results in poor comprehension. Before ESL and EFL students can read fluently, they must adopt better reading strategies.

Exercises and How They Help

Prereading capitalizes on students' experience and knowledge to help them start thinking about issues important in the story. Even though they don't know how these issues are relevant when they preread, the discussion sets their minds in motion. This is the beginning of the hypothesizing-sampling-resampling process. They are already hypothesizing (consciously or unconsciously) about what the story is about, what it has to say, its outcome, etc., and knowledge and experience are precisely what good readers use to help them hypothesize. When students read the story, the process continues: They sample to test their prereading hypothesis, and they rehypothesize and resample throughout the story. The process culminates with the *prediction exercise*, which is so important because it requires students, in predicting the story's ending, to hypothesize *consciously*.

---

[1] James Coady, "A Psycholinguistic Model of the ESL Reader," in *Reading in a Second Language: Hypotheses, Organization, and Practice*, Ronald Mackay, Bruce Barakman, and R. R. Jordan, eds. (Rowley, Mass.: Newbury House, 1979), p. 6.
[2] Coady, p. 10.

Hypothesizing applies to all levels: predicting endings, main ideas, etc.; making sense out of confusing passages or concepts; and even guessing unknown words. After the stories, two exercises are provided that involve hypothesizing at the word level: *Obtaining Meaning from Context* and the *Cloze Exercise* (in some chapters).

To see how hypothesizing works at the word level, let's take an example: Suppose I write, "The man was so *silig* he wasn't allowed to stay at the hotel." Based on the context, you might guess that *silig* meant *drunk*. However, suppose I added, "The hotel manager took one look at his clothes and turned him away." Then you would probably rehypothesize that *silig* meant *shabbily dressed*. In short, you sampled, hypothesized, resampled, and rehypothesized.

The *Reading Guide Questions* and the *Comprehension Questions* (which simply repeat the guide questions in more detail) give the student a goal to substitute for that of achieving perfect comprehension. Remember that word-by-word reading is adopted by students to achieve perfect understanding. Therefore, offering them another goal should encourage another strategy. Suppose you ask students to read an essay about blue jeans. Unless you give them a definite purpose, they will aim for perfection, give equal weight to every detail, read word by word, and comprehend poorly. On the other hand, if you ask them to read to be able to discuss why jeans are popular, they will be able to gloss over irrelevant parts, finish more quickly, and comprehend better.

The remaining exercises, *Questions for Further Discussion or Writing* and the *Optional Writing Exercises*, offer variety, interesting topics, and opportunities to practice oral and written English. Note: *Prereading* questions can also be used as writing questions after the story; rewriting story endings and other exercises not appearing in every chapter can be extended to any chapter of the teacher's choice.

Suggestions:

1. The time spent covering this book (or a given chapter) depends on the purpose. It is not necessary to do every exercise. To emphasize reading, you might limit in-class treatment to *Prereading*, the *Reading Guide Questions*, the story, the *Prediction Exercise*, and the *Comprehension Questions*—and make *Prereading* brief. *Obtaining Meaning from Context* and the *Cloze Exercise* could be assigned as homework and checked (not graded). This way, a chapter could be covered in one hour. To emphasize discussion, you might spend

two or three one-hour periods on a chapter, dividing time in the following manner: prereading, 30 minutes; reading, 10 minutes; predictions, 5 to 10 minutes; comprehension, 5 to 10 minutes (during the first period); and one or two additional periods discussing *Questions for Further Discussion or Writing.* To emphasize writing and discussion, group paragraphs based on *Questions for Further Discussion or Writing* are excellent. Students love to work together and share their writing, and the activity is extremely positive because they are the authors and experts. Expect to spend up to three hours on discussion. Concerning how many and which stories to read, I suggest the teacher decide on the number and students pick the stories.

2. Students enjoy the *Prediction Exercises*, but they are also tempted to skip ahead out of curiosity. To control this, have them close their books when they reach the *Prediction Exercise*. This is easiest to monitor if the teacher reads aloud because everyone reaches the exercise at the same time. Rewarding imaginative predictions through comments or publication is preferable to grading predictions, which might tempt students to read the story endings outside of class. By using the stories in an unpredictable order, the teacher can also discourage students from reading the story endings outside of class.

3. In an ideal world, students would switch from word-by-word reading and translation to fluent reading just by being told. In practice, however, this is rarely the case. Three methods can help the teacher facilitate the transition: (1) reading aloud by the teacher, (2) setting time limits, and (3) reading at the students' own rates. When the teacher reads aloud, the pace is relatively fast—too fast to allow students to follow along and still read one word at a time. In addition, the teacher's intonation and expression give the student input he wouldn't get from silent reading. Also, if the teacher reads aloud, the reading stops simultaneously for all students, which prevents memory loss and restlessness that result for faster readers with silent reading. An added advantage to reading aloud is that the teacher has an easier time checking to see if anyone is trying to read ahead to discover the story's ending. The only disadvantage that might be present with this method is that students could learn to rely too heavily on listening and not enough on reading. For this reason, it is recommended that reading aloud not be used exclusively. A better balance can be struck if silent reading

is used part of the time. With silent reading, however, measures must be taken to prevent students from reading one word at a time. One way to do this is with time limits. In setting time limits, teachers should use their own judgment, taking into consideration students' natural pace, the effect of the time limits on students' comprehension, and the degree of frustration the time limits create. If frustration is too great, the teacher may wish to allow students to read at their own rates. This last method should be used with caution to avoid reinforcing word-by-word reading. *Note:* For all three methods, use of dictionaries should be prohibited.

ACKNOWLEDGMENTS

For their invaluable assistance, I would like to thank Ana Laura Montaño of the computer center; Madeline Alvarez, Francisco Galletti, Anthony Lebron, Agnes Pou Rivera, Larry Fornaris, Alida Ruiz, Diane Vicens, Lydia Bermudez, Jose Conde, Carmen Diaz, Anir Diaz, Jeannie Gonzalez, Minerva Medina, Paula Melendez, Pedro Saldaña, Yolanda Rivera, and Luz Russi from my advanced composition classes; and professors Cáceres, Julie Adams, Zaida Cintron, Carmen Rosa Hernandez, Marcelo Uriaco, Edgardo Ortiz, Luis Negron, Ana Amalbert, Antonio Mansilla, Jorge Montoya, Leonardo Mora, T. E. Huber, Margarita Ortiz, and Francisca Alicea, all of Humacao University College. Special thanks are due Professor John Adams, without whose guidance and encouragement this work would never have been undertaken.

CHAPTER 1

APPEARANCES CAN BE DECEPTIVE

Prereading

Discuss the following questions before reading the story.

1. How does a person's appearance affect you? In other words, what things do you judge about a person on the basis of his or her appearance?
2. Have you ever met anyone whose appearance was *deceptive*? If so, in what sense was it deceptive?

Reading Guide Questions

Think about these questions while you read. Be prepared to answer them after you finish.

1. What person or people in this story have deceptive appearances?
2. How are appearances deceptive in this story?

The Banco Union de Venezuela on Paseo de Las Mercedes in Caracas opened at 8:00 a.m. The tellers, who attend people for deposits and withdrawals of money, were all in their places behind the long, continuous bank counter. The loan officers were all seated at their desks. The manager of the bank was standing beside the front doors to welcome people and help them as they entered the bank. The bank security guard stood holding the door open.

There were about fifty people who entered the bank at the moment the doors opened. Most of these people wanted to deposit or withdraw money from their bank accounts, so they formed a long line in front of the tellers. A few people were interested in opening new accounts, closing old accounts, or taking out loans. These people sat to wait for the loan officers to call them.

Mr. Medina was one of many loan officers in the bank. He was a tall man with a neat appearance. His hair and mustache were short and neatly trimmed. His suit was very clean, and it looked new. His tie was knotted securely at his collar and ran in a perfectly straight line down the front of his white shirt. His pants were perfectly pressed, and his shoes were so shiny that he could see his reflection in them. In short, he had an elegant appearance that was perfectly appropriate for a bank loan officer.

Mr. Medina was normally a friendly, courteous man because he worked with people and was responsible for extending credit to people by permitting them to take out loans. He was accustomed to dealing with all kinds of people, and he was proud of his public relations abilities.

This day, the first person to see Mr. Medina was an old woman who wanted to open a new savings account. It was a simple, routine situation and Mr. Medina was very friendly and efficient. He opened a new account worth two hundred dollars for the old lady in just five minutes. The woman was pleased with this fast, friendly service and she left the bank with a happy smile on her face.

Mr. Medina's second client was a young man interested in taking out a small loan. The young man dressed well and had a permanent job as an accountant. Mr. Medina completed the forms and said the bank would notify him in a few days.

At about 9:00 a.m., Mr. Medina called the third client, who walked over to his desk. This client was old, perhaps seventy years old. He wore a tattered, paint-stained coat and boots with holes in them. He told Mr. Medina that he wanted to open a savings account for $50,000. When Mr. Medina heard this, he looked at the old man's poor clothes and suspected that the old man was crazy. He paid no attention to the old man and called the next client. The old man walked out of the bank very angry.

Mr. Medina found the event mildly humorous. In fact, when he remembered it in the afternoon, he began to laugh quietly to himself.

At about 2:15 p.m., a very distinguished elderly gentleman of about retirement age entered the bank. He was wearing a suit of extraordinarily fine material and carried an exquisite polished ivory walking stick which had been shaped from the tusk of an Indian elephant. It had probably cost him several hundred dollars. The man wore a distinguished and unusually neat beard that circled his mouth and came to a subtle point below his chin.

The elderly gentleman walked slowly over to Mr. Medina's desk and tapped his walking stick on the surface of the desk. Mr. Medina looked up and immediately smiled to see such a rich client. Yes, he was quite impressed by the gentleman's appearance. The gentleman said that his name was José Soto Betancourt and that he was planning to open an account for approximately $50,000. Mr. Medina was very courteous and quickly began to look for the proper forms to complete in order to create the new account.

4   APPEARANCES CAN BE DECEPTIVE

EXERCISES

Prediction Exercise

Try to predict how the story ends. Work in groups and write your prediction in a few sentences, or offer individual predictions orally. Be prepared to justify your prediction. After all predictions have been discussed, turn to the end of the chapter to read the story's ending. In making your predictions, take into consideration the following questions:

1. How will the ending demonstrate that appearances can be deceptive?
2. Whose appearance will be deceiving? Mr. Medina's? Mr. Betancourt's? Another person's?
3. Do you think Mr. Betancourt really has $50,000?

Comprehension Questions

These questions are related to the reading guide questions that preceded the story. Answer them and be prepared to justify or explain your answers based on information from the story.

1. What are the most important or notable characteristics of Mr. Medina?
2. How does he normally treat clients?
3. Describe the appearance of the third client.
4. How does Mr. Medina treat this client? Why?
5. Describe the client who enters the bank at 2:15 p.m.
6. How does Mr. Medina treat this client? Why?
7. Who is this client?
8. Why is the old man's appearance also deceptive? Explain.
9. Is Mr. Medina's appearance also deceptive? Explain.
10. What can we learn from this story?

Questions for Further Discussion or Writing

The following questions are for discussion or writing. Choose one question and discuss it in class or write a brief, one-paragraph answer (approximately 5 to 10 sentences). You may wish to read your paragraphs in class and discuss them too.

1. Are appearances important sometimes? When? Explain.
2. Do some people place too much emphasis on appearance? Do you know such a person? Why does this person have this attitude?
3. Do you know someone who has a deceptive appearance? If so, describe the person and explain how his or her appearance is deceptive.

Optional Writing Exercise

Select a famous person with a deceptive appearance. Describe the person in a few sentences, but do not mention any names. Write your descriptions in groups and read them in the class for other groups to *guess* the identity of the person being described. In writing your description, consider the following questions: What is this person's profession—actor, writer, politician, singer, etc.? What makes the individual's appearance deceptive? Does he or she have a distinctive physical feature? What personality characteristics do most people associate with this person?

Obtaining Meaning from Context

If you do not recognize a word or expression based on its appearance, you may be able to *guess* its meaning based on context. Try to guess the meaning of the *italicized* expression. If possible, make your guess in English.

1. The *tellers*, who attend people for deposits and withdrawals of money, were all in their places behind the long, continuous bank counter.
2. His hair and mustache were short and neatly *trimmed*.
3. His tie was *knotted* securely at his collar.
4. When Mr. Medina heard this, he looked at the old man's poor clothes and suspected that the old man was *crazy*.

5. He *paid no attention* to the old man and called the next client. The old man walked out of the bank very *angry*.
6. Then he took the forms that Mr. Medina had completed and *ripped* them methodically into pieces.

STORY ENDING

When Mr. Medina was finished, the elderly gentleman congratulated him on his fine manners, courtesy, and efficiency. Then Mr. Betancourt laughed, which surprised Mr. Medina. Suddenly Mr. Betancourt removed his beard and revealed a familiar face. Mr. Medina was shocked. This distinguished gentleman was the same man who had entered the bank in the morning wearing old clothes covered with paint. He looked at Mr. Medina with penetrating eyes. Then he took the forms that Mr. Medina had completed and ripped them methodically into pieces. After that, he told Mr. Medina that he was going to take his money to Banco Royal and he walked out.

CHAPTER 2

MISS MARIA

Prereading

Discuss the following questions before reading the story.

1. What qualities do the old people you know have?
2. Who is your favorite old person? What qualities make him or her a special person?
3. What is your attitude toward old people in general (for example, respectful, impatient, pitying, admiring, etc.)? Why?

Reading Guide Questions

Think about these questions while you read. Be prepared to answer them after you finish.

1. What special qualities does Miss Maria possess?
2. How does she demonstrate these qualities?

Miss Maria was eighty years old and very thin, like a skeleton. Her hair was gray in color and sparse, like vegetation in the desert. Although she looked like a witch, she was not a bad person.

She sat in her bed in Clínica Marly in Bogotá. She was there because she felt fatigued. Sometimes she talked to people who entered the room, and sometimes she looked out the window at the traffic on Thirteenth Avenue. She saw only a blur because she was almost blind; she could only see vague, general shapes. For this reason, the nurse always fed Maria her food. One time Maria tried to find the cup of coffee without the nurse's help, but she knocked the cup over with her hand. Then the nurse told Maria to be more careful or to ask for help.

On Maria's third day there, a young woman entered the hospital and occupied the bed next to Maria's. The young woman's name was Sylvia. Sylvia was sweet and pretty, with dark hair and eyes and a round face. She had a sweet voice and was friendly to Maria. Maria liked her very much. When Sylvia's husband came to visit her, Maria always blessed him.

On Sylvia's second day in the hospital, she had an operation on her heart. Maria heard the nurses saying that the operation had not helped Sylvia's condition and that the young woman was expected to die in the next three months. A day later, Sylvia was returned to her room. Maria was not supposed to leave her bed because of her condition. It was possible for her to fall and hurt herself or to lose consciousness because of her debility. Despite her condition, Maria, through considerable effort, gradually got out of bed. With her feet, she discovered her slippers and put them on to keep her feet warm. Then she used all the strength in her old, thin arms to help her move around the bed. When she reached the end of her bed, she pushed herself toward Sylvia's bed. She almost fell! But her arms had sufficient strength to help her maintain her balance.

Maria rested a few minutes before walking farther.

After resting, she continued slowly, using her arms for support. Her legs trembled sometimes because the effort was great. When she finally reached the head of the bed, she looked into Sylvia's innocent young face and began to pray to God for Sylvia to recover from her condition. She prayed for nearly one hour, even though her legs almost collapsed. After she finished her prayer, Maria smiled upon the face of the young woman in the bed. She made a cross in the air over Sylvia to bless her. Then the old woman started back to her bed.

Three hours later, Sylvia woke up and discovered Maria on the floor. She called the nurses immediately, and they came and helped Maria into her bed. The old woman was conscious but extremely weak. She had no strength, but she had a profound smile on her face.

When Maria's doctor arrived, he examined her. While he examined her, Maria smiled and told the doctor that she knew she was dying. She said she was very happy and that she would be with God soon.

Then Maria's doctor left, and Sylvia's doctor entered. He walked over to Sylvia's bed and looked at her sadly. He was sad because the operation had not changed her condition and he expected her to die. He was thinking about this when suddenly Maria collapsed with a sigh. He ran over and took her pulse. There was no pulse! He called the nurses's station and Maria's doctor. They came quickly, but Maria was already dead.

It was strange to them that she had died with a smile on her face.

EXERCISES

Prediction Exercise

Try to predict how the story ends. Work in groups and write your prediction in a few sentences, or offer individual predictions orally. Be prepared to justify your prediction. After all predictions have been discussed, turn to the end of the chapter and read the story's ending. In making your predictions, take into consideration the following questions:

1. Will the ending of the story show why Maria died with a smile on her face?
2. Why do you think she died that way?
3. What will happen to Sylvia?

Comprehension Questions

These questions are related to the reading guide questions that preceded the story. Answer them and, when your teacher requests it, explain or justify your answers based on information from the story.

1. Why was Maria in the hospital?
2. Did she have a physical handicap? If so, what was it?
3. Why was Sylvia in the hospital?
4. Describe Sylvia.
5. How did Maria feel toward Sylvia?
6. What did Maria do to demonstrate her feelings?
7. What finally happened to Maria? To Sylvia?
8. Why do you think Maria had a smile on her face in the end?
9. What kind of person is Maria? That is, what qualities does she demonstrate?

Questions for Further Discussion or Writing

The following questions are for discussion or writing. Choose one question and discuss it in class or write a brief, one-paragraph answer (approximately 5 to 10 sentences). You may wish to read your paragraphs in class and discuss them.

1. What are some special qualities typical of old people in your country? Give examples of old people whom you know, and tell about how they have demonstrated special qualities.

2. Do old people in your country receive adequate respect, physical care, and affection? Present evidence to support your opinion.
3. Explain why you like a particular old person.

Optional Writing Exercise

Give this story a new title. In a short paragraph, defend this title. How does your title reflect the message of the story? Does it suggest any of Maria's important qualities and/or actions? Is it better than the original title? If so, why?

Obtaining Meaning from Context

If you do not recognize a word or expression based on its appearance, you may be able to *guess* its meaning based on context. Try to guess the meaning of the *italicized* expression. If possible, make your guess in English.

1. Miss Maria was eighty years old and very *thin*, like a skeleton.
2. She was only a *blur* because she was almost *blind*; she could only see vague, general shapes.
3. It was possible for her to fall and *hurt* herself or to lose consciousness because of her debility.
4. Her legs *trembled* sometimes because the effort was great.
5. The old woman was conscious but extremely *weak*. She had no strength, but she had a profound smile on her face.
6. She looked for it, and when she *found* the object, she held it up in front of her face.

STORY ENDING

After everyone had left and Maria's body had been removed, Sylvia's doctor returned to her bed. He was surprised because Sylvia was gone. He later found her out in the passageway, walking. This surprised him even more because Sylvia's condition made it impossible for her to walk. He was afraid that she would have a heart attack, but Sylvia felt strong. The doctor was amazed. This was incredible.

Finally, Sylvia decided to return to bed. Then her doctor examined her to see if her pulse and heartbeat were accelerated. To his amazement, they were normal. He did not understand. He knew the operation was not responsible. Curious, he asked Sylvia when she had begun to feel better. She said that she had felt much stronger at the moment Maria had collapsed.

The doctor felt uncomfortable. He did not want to believe there was a connection between Maria's death and the change in Sylvia's condition. Then suddenly Sylvia moved in her bed. She felt something under her pillow that made her feel uncomfortable. She looked for it, and when she found the object, she held it up in front of her face. The doctor looked shocked. It was Maria's rosary.

CHAPTER 3

THE GENERATION GAP

Prereading

Discuss the following questions before reading the story.

1. What does the term *generation gap* mean?
2. What are some of the differences in ideas that exist between younger people and older people in your country? Give examples.

Reading Guide Questions

Think about these questions while you read. Be prepared to answer them when you finish.

1. What kind of relationship exists between Raul and his grandmother?
2. What is the generation gap in this story?

Raul lay on his bed, studying his humanities textbook and listening to rock music. He had a test in humanities in three days, so he was reviewing the four chapters that would be on the test. The reason he listened to rock music was because it helped him to study and relax. He liked the music because it had a nice sound and was modern. He felt free when he listened to it. When he was tired of studying, he would try to understand the words of the songs in English, and this was fun. Later, when he wanted to study some more, it was easy to ignore the words and concentrate on his studies. In this way, the noise of the radio helped him study because it blocked out other sounds and prevented them from disturbing his concentration.

After about half an hour, Raul heard his grandmother calling him from behind the house. He turned down the radio and looked out the window. There he saw her watering her plants. When he turned the radio down, he could hear her better. She told him to stop playing the radio and start studying. He told her he liked to study with the radio on, but she did not accept that. She felt that he was not really studying, and she told him this. Because Raul respected her, he decided to try studying without the radio.

He began to read the second chapter with the radio off. It seemed easy for a few minutes, but then the neighbor lady came out and began to talk to his grandmother. She wanted to tell Raul's grandmother about her daughter who was coming from North Carolina to visit her next month. She was excited and happy. Raul tried not to listen to the conversation, but the two ladies were laughing happily. Their laughter distracted him, and he could not concentrate on his studies. Finally he had to start chapter two again because he had forgotten what it was about. About ten minutes later, the boy in the other neighbor's house turned on his radio and began to play "salsa". Raul liked "salsa" because it made him happy. He wanted to dance. Soon he found himself singing and tapping out the rhythm with his fingers. After a few minutes, he realized that he was not thinking about what he was reading and that he did not understand the chapter. He decided it was impossible to study without his radio, and so he turned it on again and started chapter two over.

Because the words of the rock music were in English, they were easy to ignore when he was thinking about something else. As a result, Raul was soon finished with chapter two. Just as he began to read chapter three, his grandmother called him. When he heard her voice, he turned the radio down again. One more time, his grandmother told him that he could not study with the radio on. Even though Raul knew this was not true, he could not say anything to his grandmother because he did not want to offend her.

After he had turned off the radio, Raul found a towel and went to the bathroom to take a shower. When he finished his shower, he put on new clothes and cologne. Then his grandmother saw him and asked where he was going. Raul told her he was going to his girlfriend's house. She said that he had not studied very long, but Raul told her he didn't have much homework. His grandmother reminded him that his grades last semester had not been good. Raul said that he was doing better this semester. Then he asked for his grandmother's blessing and went out.

During the time he was with his girlfriend, Raul was very happy. They understood each other because they were both young. They both liked to study while listening to the radio, too, but they did not study often together because they preferred to talk about their feelings of love and the future they would share.

The day of the test, Raul woke up at 5:00 a.m. There was nobody awake; everyone was sleeping. Everything was quiet. Raul turned on the light in his room and opened his humanities book to chapter three. He began to read fast because he had a test at 8:00 a.m.

EXERCISES

Prediction Exercise

Try to predict how the story ends. Work in groups and write your prediction in a few sentences, or offer individual predictions orally. Be prepared to justify your prediction. After all predictions have been discussed, turn to the end of the chapter and read the story's ending. In making your predictions, take into consideration the following questions:

1. How will Raul do on the test?
2. Do you think he will continue to study with the radio on?
3. Will his grandmother change her attitude toward his studying with the radio on? Why or why not?
4. Will Raul change his study habits? Why or why not?

Comprehension Questions

These questions are related to the reading guide questions that preceded the story. Answer them and be prepared to justify or explain your answers (upon your teacher's request) with information from the story.

1. How does Raul prefer to study? Why?
2. How does his grandmother feel about this? Why?
3. Does Raul respect his grandmother? Explain.
4. Does his grandmother have a helpful attitude? Explain.
5. What kind of relationship does Raul have with his girlfriend?
6. How does the generation gap between Raul and his grandmother affect him?

Questions for Further Discussion or Writing

The following questions are for discussion or writing. Choose one question and discuss it in class or write a brief, one-paragraph answer (approximately 5 to 10 sentences). You may wish to read your paragraphs in class and discuss them, too.

1. Have you ever had an experience similar to Raul's? If so, describe

your experience and comment on it. Were you able to resolve your differences with the other person?
2. Have you ever created obstacles for someone by trying to be helpful? If so, describe the incident.
3. Describe your study habits. Do you like to listen to music while you study? If so, what kind and why? Do you feel that your study habits are effective? Explain. Do your parents accept your study habits?
4. Choose a topic (dress, music, eating habits, dating and marriage, family unity versus individual identity, etc.). Explore the differences in ideas that exist between younger and older people with respect to this topic.

Optional Writing Exercise

Rewrite the ending of "The Generation Gap." In the process, consider the following questions: Should Raul change his study habits? Should his grandmother change her attitude? If so, what will make her change it? Will the generation gap be reduced?

Obtaining Meaning from Context:

If you do not recognize a word or expression based on its appearance, you may be able to *guess* its meaning based on context. Try to guess the meaning of the *italicized* expression. If possible, make your guess in English.

1. In this way, the noise of the radio helped him to study because it blocked out other sounds and prevented them from *disturbing* his concentration.
2. Finally he had to start chapter two again because he had *forgotten* what it was about.
3. They both liked to study while listening to the radio, too, but they did not study often together because they preferred to talk about their feelings of love and the future they would *share*.
4. There was nobody *awake*; everyone was sleeping.
5. He had no time to finish studying. Raul closed his book and *hurried* to get ready.

6. Then she assumed that he had *flunked*, and she began to shout and criticize him.

STORY ENDING

Raul sat up suddenly in his bed. He rubbed his eyes and looked at the alarm clock. It was 7:30 a.m. Then he looked at his humanities book and saw that he had not finished the third chapter. Now he had only thirty minutes to take a shower and catch a bus to the college. He had no time to finish studying. Raul closed his book and hurried to get ready.

When the bus arrived at the college, Raul jumped off and ran to his classroom. Even though he was late, the teacher was happy to see him. He gave Raul a test, and Raul sat down and began to read. The first part of the test was easy because Raul had read the material and understood what he read, but the last third of the test was difficult because he had not read that part of the book.

When he arrived home, his grandmother was waiting for him. She immediately asked how he had done on his test. Raul told her nothing. Then she assumed that he had flunked, and she began to shout and criticize him. She said that he was irresponsible and lazy. Raul put away his books, took a shower, and went to his girlfriend's house. They talked together about getting married and having a family, but Raul was thinking about the test and his grandmother.

CHAPTER 4

CARMEN'S TWO BOYFRIENDS

Prereading

Discuss the following questions before reading the story.

1. What does the title, "Carmen's Two Boyfriends," mean to you? What decision does it imply? What questions does it make you ask?

Reading Guide Questions

Think about these questions while you read. Be prepared to answer them when you finish.

1. What attractive qualities does each young man possess?
2. Which boyfriend does Carmen prefer?

Carmen Gonzalez was eighteen years old. She studied Secretarial Science at Huertas Community College, and, in her free time, she liked to dance and go to parties. Her family was middle class.

Carmen had two boyfriends. That is, there were two young men that she was interested in. She liked them both, but she could not decide which she preferred.

One boyfriend, Roberto, was from a poor family. Although his parents had no money, Roberto was working at a supermarket to earn money to pay for his education. He studied at the same school as Carmen, but he was studying accounting. Roberto worked all day Saturday and Sunday and he studied in the evenings, Monday through Friday. He usually saw Carmen at school, but some Saturday nights they went to a movie or a discothèque.

The other young man's name was Gilberto. His family was wealthy; consequently, Gilberto was able to drive around in a Ferrari. Because he was brilliant, he found law school easy and had lots of free time. During his free time he liked to read and play tennis. Gilberto was courteous. For example, when he and Carmen went to a restaurant, he held her chair for her. Frequently they had conversations about values and life philosophies. Gilberto was very understanding and seemed to share many of Carmen's ideas.

Carmen did not want Roberto and Gilberto to meet, and she did not want her parents to know she had two boyfriends. To protect her secret, she convinced Roberto that her father was a monster who would not allow her to have a boyfriend. This way she could see Gilberto at her house and Roberto in other places. This would keep the two young men apart.

One Sunday Carmen was sitting on her porch, thinking about Roberto and Gilberto. When she heard Roberto's car, she was surprised and nervous. Fortunately her parents were not home at the moment, but they might return soon. Roberto had a red rose for Carmen. They sat on the porch and talked. Carmen was secretly happy, but she acted serious. She criticized Roberto for behaving capriciously and foolishly. She tried to make him leave, but he insisted on talking with her for a few minutes. After they had talked for awhile, Carmen went to the kitchen to make some lemonade. She planned to give Roberto something to drink and then persuade him to leave. While she was in the kitchen, she heard a car stop in front of the house.

EXERCISES

Prediction Exercise

Try to predict how the story ends. Work in groups and write your prediction in a few sentences, or offer individual predictions orally. Be prepared to justify your prediction. After all predictions have been discussed, turn to the end of the chapter and read the story's ending. In making your predictions, take into consideration the following questions:

1. Whose car stopped in front of Carmen's house?
2. Will her secret be discovered?
3. Will Carmen be happy in the end?

Comprehension Questions

These questions are related to the reading guide questions that preceded the story. Answer them and be prepared to justify your answers when your teacher requests it.

1. Describe Gilberto.
2. Describe Roberto.
3. How are they different?

4. Which young man does Carmen prefer and why?

Questions for Further Discussion or Writing

The following questions are for discussion or writing. Choose one question and discuss it in class or write a brief, one-paragraph answer (approximately 5 to 10 sentences). You may wish to read your paragraphs in class and discuss them, too.

1. If you were Carmen, which boyfriend would you choose and why?
2. What is the most important quality(ies) you desire in a boy or girlfriend, and why?

Optional Writing Exercise

Rewrite the ending of "Carmen's Two Boyfriends." In doing so, consider the following questions: How should Gilberto and Roberto react when they discover Carmen's secret? Should Carmen be happy in the end? Do her parents discover her secret?

Obtaining Meaning from Context

If you do not recognize a word or expression based on its appearance, you may be able to *guess* its meaning based on context. Try to guess the meaning of the *italicized* expression. If possible, make your guess in English.

1. Roberto was working at a supermarket to *earn* money to pay for his education.
2. His family was *wealthy*; consequently, Gilberto was able to drive around in a Ferrari.
3. To protect her secret, she convinced Roberto that her father was a monster who would not *allow* her to have a boyfriend.
4. She criticized Roberto for *behaving* capriciously and *foolishly*.
5. She tried to make him *leave*, but he insisted on talking with her for a few minutes.
6. ... she began to cry. Roberto and Gilberto interpreted this behavior as evidence of Carmen's *guilt*, and they left.

7. Then she began to cry because she thought Roberto would never *forgive* her.

STORY ENDING

When she reached the porch, Roberto and Gilberto were both there. From their faces, it was evident that they had already discovered Carmen's secret. They looked at her for an explanation, but Carmen was so nervous that she began to cry. Roberto and Gilberto interpreted this behavior as evidence of Carmen's guilt, and they left. Carmen was alone, crying because she thought that she would probably never see Roberto or Gilberto again.

A few months passed, and Carmen graduated from Huertas Community College with an Associate's Degree in Secretarial Science. She got a job working as a secretary and became more mature and responsible. Finally, one day she decided to call Gilberto. She apologized for her dishonesty and explained that she had been trying to decide who she preferred. She said she admired Gilberto and considered him a good friend but that she loved Roberto. Then she began to cry because she thought Roberto would never forgive her.

Gilberto called Roberto and told him what Carmen had said.

The next day, Carmen was on the porch. She was thinking about Roberto and she began to cry. Suddenly, she heard a familiar car approaching. She looked up because she could not believe her ears. It was true! Roberto's car had stopped in front of Carmen's house. He came onto the porch and they began to talk seriously.

Finally, Carmen and Roberto embraced. Then Carmen took Roberto inside to meet her mother and father.

CHAPTER 5

THE MISTAKE

Prereading

Discuss the following questions before reading the story.

1. Are you critical of your parents? Your brothers and sisters? Your friends? Your teachers?
2. Are you more critical of people you like or people you don't like? Why?
3. Where do you criticize others? In public? In private? To their faces? When they are not present?
4. How do you feel when you are criticizing someone? Do you feel powerful, angry, uncomfortable?
5. Who criticizes you and how do you feel when you are criticized?

Reading Guide Questions

Think about these questions while you read. Be prepared to answer them after you finish.

1. How does Julio's mother treat him? How does Julio feel about this?
2. How does Julio change as a result of this treatment?

Julio was washing the dishes in the kitchen sink. He wanted to help his mother, Irma. He knew that she was busy. She had taken a job recently in a cigar factory because Julio's father had abandoned them. She was always busy working at home or at the factory. Julio felt good because he was helping her. When he finished doing the dishes, his mother came into the kitchen. She looked serious as she examined the dishes carefully. They all seemed to shine brilliantly because they were so clean. Julio was waiting for her opinion. He was smiling. Suddenly she saw a speck of dry tomato sauce on a plate. It was a very small speck, but that was not important to Irma. Immediately, she criticized him for his negligence. Julio felt terrible, but he was silent.

The next day, Julio went to the grocery store for his mother. She asked him to bring her rice, beans, tomato sauce, pork chops, potatoes, lettuce, milk, bread, frozen orange juice, and doughnuts. When Julio got to the store, he looked thoroughly for exactly what his mother wanted. He knew that she liked Holsum bread, for example. She would not be happy if he bought another brand of bread. He also knew that she preferred medium-grain rice. But that day there was no medium-grain rice in the store. Julio gave considerable thought to this problem before he finally decided to buy short-grain rice. He felt that this was a good decision.

However, when Julio got home, he felt tense. He began to empty the grocery bag in the kitchen. Then he started to put everything in its place. While he was working, his mother came into the kitchen. She saw the bag of rice on the kitchen counter and began to scream at him. She said he should never have bought short-grain rice and she called him an idiot.

Julio was so offended that he tried to defend himself, but Irma just wouldn't listen. Julio finally walked out of the house.

During the weekend, Julio planned to go fishing with a friend, but he was supposed to clean the yard first. His mother asked him to cut the grass and collect the cut grass in a plastic garbage bag. He was also supposed to collect all dead leaves in the bag. Julio enjoyed working in the yard. It was nice to work outside in the open air. The breeze was cool and made him feel calm. He was able to think his private thoughts without interruption.

When he finished cutting the grass and collecting the grass and leaves, his mother came outside to inspect his work, as usual. The work was perfect. There was not one leaf on the ground, and all the cut grass had been neatly collected. For a minute, Irma was silent. Then she told him that the work was acceptable, but she wanted him to sweep and mop the carport.

Julio could not believe it. His friend was going to arrive in a few minutes. If he swept and mopped the carport, he would not be able to go fishing. He had been planning this fishing trip since Monday. He really wanted to go. Julio decided to appeal to his mother. He reminded her about his fishing trip with Rolando.

His mother thought for a minute. She said she had forgotten the trip. She said it was all right for him to go if he promised to clean the carport when he arrived home. Julio was so happy that he embraced his mother. He forgot all the times that she had criticized him. Then he went inside to change his clothes.

When Julio got home, it was late. It was nine o'clock at night and very dark. He turned on the light in the carport and tried to sweep it carefully, but the light was not very good. He did the best work possible, but he could not see very well. The next morning, his mother woke up early and went to the carport to look for imperfections. This time her job was not difficult. There was dirt in the corners and the floor did not look very shiny. But Irma was quiet.

When Julio came home from school, he was excited. He had done a science project and his project was selected as the best in the school. It would be entered in competition with other projects in the town. When he finished telling his mother the news, she looked at him and smiled. Julio thought she was proud of him. However, Irma didn't talk about the science project. Instead, she criticized the work Julio had done on the carport.

After that, Julio didn't even try to do things. When his mother asked him to do something, he said he was sick or he simply ignored her. Irma became worried. She was afraid that Julio was really sick. She took him to see a doctor, but the doctor said that Julio was strong and healthy.

A week later, Julio's science project was selected as the best project in the town. His science teacher wanted Julio to enter his project in a national competition. When he called Julio, however, Julio said that he was not interested. He did not talk about it. He just hung up the telephone.

During the next two weeks, Julio's grades in school went down. He was normally an A student in science and a C student in his other subjects. During those two weeks, he got all D's and F's. His teachers tried to talk to him, but Julio was silent. They called his mother and talked to her, but she was confused about Julio, too. When she talked to him, he said that he was sick. This situation continued.

One day Julio and his mother were outside sitting on the porch. His mother saw a friend on the other side of the street. She smiled and waved at the friend. Julio felt sad and jealous. Why didn't his mother smile at him? Julio's mother decided to go visit her friend, and she started to cross the street. Suddenly a crazy driver turned the corner. Julio ran toward his mother in the street. The car came toward them at fifty miles per hour. Julio acted rapidly. He pushed his mother.

EXERCISES

Prediction Exercise

Try to predict how the story ends. Work in groups and write your prediction in a few sentences, or offer individual predictions orally. Be

28 THE MISTAKE

prepared to justify your prediction. After all predictions have been discussed, turn to the end of the chapter and read the story's ending. In making your predictions, take into consideration the following questions:

1. Why did Julio push his mother?
2. Will Julio or his mother be hit by the speeding car?
3. How will the end of the story tell us what the mistake was?

Comprehension Questions

These questions are related to the reading guide questions that preceded the story. Answer them and be prepared to justify or explain your answers based on information from the story.

1. How would you describe Julio? Why?
2. What qualities would you say his mother has? Why?
3. What different things does Julio do for his mother? Does he do a good job?
4. What kind of student is Julio normally?
5. What honor does he receive?
6. How does his mother react to this honor?
7. How does Julio's attitude toward school change? Why?
8. How does his attitude toward life change?
9. How does the story end?
10. What was the mistake?

Questions for Further Discussion or Writing

The following questions are for discussion or writing. Choose one question and discuss it in class or write a brief, one-paragraph answer (approximately 5 to 10 sentences). You may wish to read your paragraphs in class and discuss them.

1. Have you ever had an experience similar to Julio's? Who criticized you? Where? When? Why? How did you feel?
2. Pretend that you are a friend of Julio and his mother and you

want to help them. What would you say to Irma? Would you mention Julio's good qualities? Would you talk to Julio?

Optional Writing Exercise

Working in groups, give this story a new title. In a short paragraph, defend your choice by explaining how it reflects the message, people, and/or events of the story. Is your title better than the original? If so, why?

Obtaining Meaning from Context

If you do not recognize a word or expression based on its appearance, you may be able to *guess* its meaning based on context. Try to guess the meaning of the *italicized* expression. If possible, make your guess in English.

1. If he *swept and mopped* the carport, he would not be able to go fishing.
2. There was *dirt* in the corners and the floor did not look very shiny.
3. . . . she looked at him and smiled. Julio thought she was *proud of him*.
4. She was afraid that Julio was really *sick*. She took him to see a doctor. . . .
5. He did not talk about it. He just *hung up the telephone*.

STORY ENDING

His mother fell to the ground, and the car went by. Julio had saved his mother's life. Irma stood up and began screaming at Julio because he had pushed her very hard and had gotten her dress dirty. Suddenly, Julio screamed back. He said that he was going crazy because she always criticized him and never demonstrated love. Then Irma's facial expression changed. For a moment, she was quiet, thinking. Then she spoke. She explained that she had been unhappy since Julio's father had deserted them. She apologized. Through tears, she said that she would never criticize him unjustly again. Then Julio and his mother embraced.

CHAPTER 6

MEXICO IS BEAUTIFUL

Prereading

Discuss the following questions before reading the story.

1. Name some things that are beautiful to you. Can feelings be beautiful? Is beauty always physical?
2. Do the people in your country have special qualities that make them beautiful? Explain. Give examples.

Reading Guide Questions

Think about these questions while you read. Be prepared to answer them when you finish.

1. What different kinds of beauty are present in this story?
2. What is the greatest example of beauty in the story?

When I was living in Mexico as a graduate student, my fellow students and I took frequent trips to the famous places of Mexico. We were fond of the beach, the pyramids, the cathedrals, the art museums, and the mountains. One weekend we decided to visit Citlaltepec, also known as Orizaba. This is a volcanic mountain and the highest peak in Mexico. It reaches an altitude of 18,700 feet and is part of the Transversal Volcanic Mountain Range in the southern part of Mexico. The mountains are of varied appearance. Sometimes you can see volcanic ash and projections where the volcanoes have erupted. Other times you can see fresh streams. Some of the surface is covered with salt and rock. In the hollow cavities between the mountain peaks, there is extreme erosion of the soil because of the rivers that flow into the oceans. Above eight thousand feet, there are great forests of pine trees. At lower altitudes, the forests are composed of pines and oaks and the earth below the trees is covered with moss and ferns.

It was a beautiful day for a visit to the mountains. The sky was azure blue, the sun shone brilliantly, and there was a pleasant breeze. My friends and I hopped into my old car and started toward the mountains. We were singing old songs and laughing and telling jokes when suddenly we heard a sound like a pistol shot. We slowed down the car and pulled off the road to examine the tires. Unfortunately what we suspected was true: We had a flat tire. But the worst news was that the spare tire was no good! It was very old and had no air. What a terrible thing to happen on such a beautiful day. Finally, we decided to start walking toward the nearest service station for help.

EXERCISES

Prediction Exercise

Try to predict how the story ends. Work in groups and write your prediction in a few sentences, or offer individual predictions orally. Be prepared to justify your prediction. After all predictions have been discussed, turn to the end of the chapter and read the story's ending. In making your predictions, take into consideration the following questions:

1. Will the graduate students reach Mt. Citlaltepec?
2. How will the ending show that Mexico is beautiful?

Comprehension Questions

These questions are related to the reading guide questions that preceded the story. Answer them and justify your answers based on information from the story when your teacher requests it.

1. Where do the friends decide to go on the weekend?
2. What problem interrupts the trip?
3. Who helps them? Describe the person physically and in terms of personality.
4. Did the person who helped them accept money? What did he consider his payment?
5. What two different kinds of beauty are described in this story? Which one is greater and why?

Questions for Further Discussion or Writing

The following questions are for discussion or writing. Choose one question and discuss it in class or write a brief, one-paragraph answer (approximately 5 to 10 sentences). You may wish to read your paragraphs in class and discuss them.

1. *For discussion*: Why is your country beautiful? Consider the beauty of the land, the historical and cultural sites, the music, the literature, the customs, the people, etc. *For writing*: choose one specific custom, historical site, or other beautiful thing and describe or explain its beauty.

2. *For discussion*: What things detract from the beauty of your country and why? What, if anything, can be done to change them? *For writing*: Choose something specific that detracts from the beauty of your country and answer the same questions.

Optional Writing Exercise

Select a famous person whom you consider beautiful. Describe him or her in a few sentences. Do your writing in groups and share it with the class. Do not mention the identity of the person; this way, the other groups can guess it. In writing your description, you may wish to give some hint about the identity of the individual (for example, profession, honors received, distinguishing characteristic, etc.). In addition, you should say why the person is beautiful and present evidence.

Obtaining Meaning from Context

If you do not recognize a word or expression based on its appearance, you may be able to *guess* its meaning based on context. Try to guess the meaning of the *italicized* expression. If possible, make your guess in English.

1. We were *fond of* the beach, the pyramids, the cathedrals, the art museums, and the mountains.
2. This is a volcanic mountain and the highest *peak* in Mexico.
3. In the hollow cavities between the mountain peaks, there is extreme erosion of the soil because of the rivers that *flow* into the oceans.
4. Unfortunately what we suspected was true: We had a *flat* tire.
5. The road where we walked had no *shade*, and the sun was *striking* us directly.

6. He said that the mountains were very beautiful but not as beautiful as the old man. We all *agreed*.

STORY ENDING

While we walked, we thought about water and beer and other cool things to drink. The road where we walked had no shade, and the sun was striking us directly. This made us feel extremely hot. After about half an hour, an old truck pulled off the road in front of us and stopped. When we reached the truck, an old Mexican man got out of the truck. He was about seventy-five years old and had a gray beard and hair. His clothes smelled of farm animals, which caused us to make funny faces. However, his smile was big and genuine and his eyes shone brilliantly when he talked.

We tried to communicate in Spanish, but he did not understand because our Spanish was not very good. Then he surprised us by speaking a few words of English. We explained our situation and he smiled. He walked back to the car with us and helped remove the tire. Then he took us to a service station where the tire was repaired and took us back to our car. When we offered to pay him, he said no thank you. He smiled. Then we smiled. This, he said, was the best way that we could pay him—with our smiles. We thanked him. After that, he got in his truck and drove away.

When we arrived at Citlaltepec, we got out of the car and looked up at the mountain and remarked how beautiful it was. Then one of my friends said something that was true. He said that the mountains were very beautiful, but not as beautiful as the old man. We all agreed.

CHAPTER 7

THE TV FRIEND

Prereading

Discuss the following questions before reading the story.

1. What effects does TV have on children?
2. Which programs do you think have positive effects? Which programs do you think have negative effects?
3. How do children perceive TV heroes?

Reading Guide Questions

Think about these questions while you read. Be prepared to answer them when you finish.

1. How does TV affect Angel?
2. What is the result?

Angel was an eight-year-old boy who lived in San Carlos Centro, Argentina. His father worked on a small wheat farm owned by an Italian immigrant, and his mother did domestic work—sewing, cleaning, etc. His father was always tired when he returned home from work, and his mother was always busy.

In school, Angel was very attentive and courteous. Though he was of average intelligence, his teacher usually sent home glowing reports about him because his behavior and participation were quite good.

In their house, Angel's family had a recently acquired TV. It was small and old and the picture was black and white, but Angel thought that it was wonderful. Soon he was spending hours in front of the TV. He became so involved with the programs that he thought they were real. Sometimes he even talked to the TV.

One day Angel's teacher asked the students to give oral presentations. She asked each youngster to bring something to class to tell the other students about. Angel thought about the assignment and decided that he would like to take the TV to the classroom to talk about; however, he knew that his mother and father would not let him do that. What would he take?

The day of the oral presentations arrived. The children went into the school. Each child was carrying an object in his hands. Many of them were talking excitedly about the toy or other object they had brought for their presentations. They all had something to talk about. Melissa had her favorite doll, Victor had a toy airplane, and Carlos had a set of paints. Then one of the children turned to Angel and asked him what he was going to talk about. Angel was not carrying anything. He smiled and told the other children that he had something special to talk about. He said it was going to be a surprise.

Soon the teacher began the class. She began with some arithmetic and then some language skills and finally she came to the fun part. The first student to talk was Sandra. She had brought a guitar. She was very excited because her father had promised to give her guitar lessons. The second person to talk was Victor. He explained that he liked airplanes because his father was an airplane mechanic in the past. Finally Angel's turn came. He stood in front of the class with nothing in his hands. The teacher felt sorry for Angel because she thought that he was too poor to have something to bring to class. But then Angel began to talk. He extended his hand as if he were introducing someone. He talked about a friend and explained that the friend had special abilities. He could fly and he was very powerful. All the time, Angel kept looking at the empty space beside him as if it were occupied by a living person. Everyone in the class, including the teacher, was perplexed.

One day a note arrived at Angel's house. It was a note from his teacher. She wanted to see Angel's parents at the school. She said that she was worried about Angel. Angel's parents had a lot of work and they didn't want to go to the school. They talked to Angel, and he said that there was no problem. Because of this, his parents decided to ignore the teacher's note.

On Saturday his mother was sewing a dress for a customer when she heard Angel talking. She looked outside and saw that Angel was alone. However, he was talking to the empty space beside him. Apparently, he had an imaginary friend. She thought for a minute. She remembered the teacher's note. But then she laughed to herself. Many children have imaginary friends, she thought. Then she went on with her sewing.

An hour later, she heard her husband shouting something to Angel. She went outside to find out what was happening.

EXERCISES

Prediction Exercise

Try to predict how the story ends. Work in groups and write your predictions in a few sentences, or offer individual predictions orally. Be prepared to justify your prediction. After all predictions have been discussed, turn to the end of the chapter and read the story's ending. In making predictions, consider the following questions:

1. Why was Angel's father shouting at him?
2. How do you think the TV friend will be important in the ending?
3. Do you think that Angel's imaginary friend is unimportant, as his mother believes?

Comprehension Questions

These questions are related to the reading guide questions that preceded the story. Answer them and justify your answers when your teacher requests it.

1. Describe Angel.
2. How did he feel about TV?
3. How did TV affect him? Give evidence.
4. What did Angel discuss in his oral presentation in school?
5. How did his teacher react?
6. How did his parents react to his odd behavior? Was his father aware of Angel's friend?
7. What finally happened to Angel and how was this related to the imaginary friend?

Questions for Further Discussion or Writing

The following questions are for discussion or writing. Choose one question and discuss it in class or write a brief, one-paragraph answer (approximately 5 to 10 sentences). You may wish to read your paragraphs in class and discuss them.

1. What programs do you feel have a negative influence on children or on people in general? Why do you feel these programs have a bad influence—insensitive treatment of sex, violence, lack of realism, other reasons?
2. Which programs have a positive influence and why?
3. What practices do you follow at home to reduce the negative effects of TV? If you have no concrete method for handling this problem, what ideas occur to you? For example, would you limit the time spent watching TV? Would you select children's programs for them? Why or why not?

Optional Writing Exercise

Select a TV character (cartoon character, animal, supporting actor or actress, etc.) and write a short description (25 words) in your group. Put as many details as possible, including impressive characteristics, notable accomplishments, etc. The groups in the class can try to guess the identity of this character.

Obtaining Meaning from Context

If you do not recognize a word or expression based on its appearance, you may be able to *guess* its meaning based on context. Try to guess the meaning of the *italicized* expression. If possible, make your guess in English.

1. Though he was of average intelligence, his teacher usually sent home *glowing* reports because his behavior and participation were quite good.
2. She asked each *youngster* to bring something to class to tell the other students about.
3. All the time, Angel kept looking at the empty space beside him as if it were occupied by a living person. Everyone in the class, including the teacher, was *perplexed*.
4. She [the teacher] said that she was *worried* about Angel.

STORY ENDING

When she arrived outside, she saw that her husband looked frightened. This was unusual because he was a courageous man. He had worked with bulls and had never been afraid. He was looking at something on the roof. She looked up at the roof to see what it was. On the roof was her son, Angel. He had a bathroom towel tied around his neck like a cape. He was talking, but she could not see anyone else on the roof. Suddenly, Angel jumped from the roof. He held out his arms as if to fly, but he fell directly to the ground and broke his neck. He died.

CHAPTER 8

THE FATAL FRIENDSHIP

Prereading

Discuss these questions before reading the story.

1. Think about all of your friends. Are they all true friends? What makes a good friendship?
2. Have you ever had a friend who was disloyal, manipulative, exploitative, insincere, or a bad influence? Elaborate.

Reading Guide Questions

Think about these questions while you read. Be prepared to answer them when you finish.

1. What qualities does Guillermo have? Is he a good friend?
2. How would you characterize Rene's friendship with Guillermo? With Ivonne?
3. In addition to Guillermo, Rene, and Ivonne, there is a fourth "friend." Identify this friend. What is the fatal friendship?

Guillermo was an intelligent boy. On his first day of kindergarten, his teacher recognized Guillermo's intelligence easily because Guillermo was the only child who could read; no other boy or girl in the kindergarten had this ability.

As Guillermo grew older, he became increasingly successful in school. When he was in elementary school, he got almost all A's. When he reached high school, he was recognized as one of the most intelligent youths in the city.

In addition to academic ability, he also had athletic ability. He was the best hitter on the high school baseball team, with a batting average of .353. He was an excellent basketball player, too; he averaged sixteen points per game and five assists and was the playmaker of the team.

Besides being intelligent and athletic, Guillermo had considerable talent for music. He played the guitar, the piano, and the cuatro and had a marvelous voice.

In short, he was a fortunate young man—intelligent, athletic, and musically gifted. But that was not all. In addition to these three gifts, Guillermo had another positive quality: He was handsome. He had green eyes, a well-proportioned nose, a shapely mouth, and a strong chin. His body was athletic and graceful. He was five feet, eight inches tall, with powerful muscles in his shoulders, chest, and arms, and he had a slender waist and muscular legs.

But Guillermo had a serious problem—he was insecure. He was insecure because the relationship between his mother and father was turbulent. His mother and father were always fighting. As a consequence of this bad relationship between his parents, Guillermo was afraid to become involved with a girl. He was a sensitive boy, and he was afraid that a relationship between himself and a girl might be as bad as the one between his mother and father.

One day a friend presented Guillermo to a boy named Rene. Rene was an older boy—eighteen, compared to Guillermo, who was sixteen. In Guillermo's opinion, Rene was strange. He had long, straight hair like a girl's, wore his clothes carelessly, and smoked unusual cigarettes. These cigarettes were unusual because they did not look like the cigarettes that are sold in the supermarket. They were fat in the middle and thin at the ends. Rene said he rolled them at home with a very special "tobacco." Guillermo recognized the irony in Rene's voice. When he asked, Rene admitted that the cigarettes contained marijuana and asked Guillermo if he wanted to smoke one.

Guillermo knew that smoking marijuana could be dangerous. He had read in science class that marijuana caused hallucinations and that frequent use can cause memory loss and paranoia. He told this to Rene, but Rene just laughed. He told Guillermo that the science textbooks were wrong because he had smoked marijuana for four years without any problems.

Guillermo was still not convinced, but then something happened. A very pretty girl came up to Rene and gave him a kiss. Rene received this kiss casually. His self-confident manner with this girl impressed Guillermo. Then Rene shared his marijuana cigarette with the girl, whose name was Ivonne. She gave Guillermo a special smile and offered him the cigarette. Rene started to tell her that Guillermo was square, but Guillermo quickly extended his hand and took the cigarette. He thanked Ivonne.

The next day, when Guillermo went to see Rene again, Ivonne was there. When she saw Guillermo, she walked over to him and gave him a big kiss. The three young people smoked a few joints. After that, Guillermo and Ivonne went away to be alone.

During the next few weeks, Guillermo spent all of his free time with Ivonne. They went everywhere together—to parks, museums, the movies. Guillermo discovered that Ivonne was a sensitive, intelligent girl, but he also recognized that she was sometimes incoherent in conversation.

One day, he noticed some marks on her arm. He questioned her, but she refused to answer him. Her refusal made him infer that she was taking other drugs besides marijuana. He went to Rene for help, but Rene only laughed. He said Ivonne was a prostitute who only wanted Guillermo's money for drugs. Guillermo returned to her to offer help. He said that his father would help her get medical attention, but Ivonne laughed bitterly and pushed him out the door.

Guillermo felt destroyed. He had never cared about a girl before, and he felt something special for Ivonne. He was so depressed that when he got home he went directly to his bedroom and locked the door.

When Guillermo did not come to supper, his father decided to find out the reason why.

EXERCISES

Prediction Exercise

Try to predict how the story ends. Work in groups to write brief predictions, or offer individual predictions orally. Be prepared to justify your prediction. After all predictions have been discussed, turn to the end of the chapter and read the story's ending. In making predictions, consider the following questions:

1. Is Guillermo so depressed that he has taken his life?
2. If he does not take his life, what will happen to Guillermo's relationship with Ivonne?
3. How will the ending justify the title?

Comprehension Questions

These questions are related to the reading guide questions that preceded the story. Answer them and justify your answers when your teacher requests it.

1. What abilities does Guillermo have?
2. What is his most negative quality and why does he have this quality?

3. What qualities does Rene have and which one impresses Guillermo?
4. Why does Guillermo become involved with drugs?
5. Are his feelings for Ivonne sincere?
6. What is the fatal friendship?
7. How does Guillermo react to Ivonne's tragedy? What good things does he do?

Questions for Further Discussion or Writing

The following questions are for writing or discussion. Choose one and discuss it or write a brief paragraph about it. You may wish to share your paragraphs.

1. What attracts people to drugs? Do they believe that drugs make them sexier, more intelligent, more powerful? Do they think drugs are glamorous? Support your answers.
2. What is the truth about drugs? Do they have positive effects on physical appearance, intelligence, personality, athletic prowess? Cite examples to support your opinion.

Optional Writing Exercise

If you do not like the title of this story, give it another title which you consider more appropriate. Justify your choice of a title in a few sentences.

Obtaining Meaning from Context

If you do not recognize a word or expression based on its appearance, you may be able to *guess* its meaning based on context. Try to guess the meaning of the *italicized* expression. If possible, make your guess in English.

1. As Guillermo grew older, he became increasingly *successful* in school. When he was in elementary school, he got almost all A's.
2. Rene started to tell her that Guillermo was *square*, but Guillermo quickly extended his hand and took the cigarette.
3. The three young people smoked a few *joints*.

4. He said that his father would help her get medical attention, but Ivonne laughed *bitterly* and pushed him out the door.
5. The second time, he still did not answer. Finally Mr. Velazquez *pounded* desperately on the door.
6. She had died of an *overdose* of heroin.
7. Guillermo cried when he heard the news. However, after *mourning* sufficiently, he acted with great composure and maturity.
8. As a result, Rene was arrested for *pandering* and possession of controlled substances.
9. Second, when he attended Ivonne's *wake*, he had enough control of his emotions to talk with Ivonne's parents and console them.

STORY ENDING

The first time his father knocked, Guillermo did not answer. The second time, he still did not answer. Finally Mr. Valezquez pounded desperately on the door. At that moment, Guillermo opened the door.

He and his father talked, which made Guillermo feel better. His father promised to help Guillermo if possible, but he told the boy to be prepared for a difficult battle. Guillermo said that he would go see Ivonne the next day.

That night, the police found Ivonne's body in Rene's apartment. She had died of an overdose of heroin. Guillermo cried when he heard the news. However, after mourning sufficiently, he acted with great composure and maturity. First, he told the police narcotics experts everything he knew. As a result, Rene was arrested for pandering and possession of controlled substances. Second, when he attended Ivonne's wake, he had enough control of his emotions to talk with Ivonne's parents and console them.

His experience made Guillermo aware of his profound love of human life and helped him to decide to study sociology.

CHAPTER 9

THE VIDEO GAME GENIUS

Prereading

Discuss these questions before reading.

1. Playing video games is a common pastime among young people. What is your opinion of these games?
2. Do you play electronic video games? If so, how do you feel when you play?
3. Do you consider these games entertainment or a vice? Explain.

Reading Guide Questions

Think about these questions while you read. Be prepared to answer them when you finish.

1. How does playing video games affect José Gabriel?
2. Why is he a video game genius?
3. Does playing video games become a vice for José Gabriel?

José Gabriel was nineteen years old. He had a handsome face that reflected an Indian ancestry: pronounced cheekbones and dark, brilliant eyes. He was an intelligent young Peruvian with a consuming interest in mathematics, and he had even published a paper in "Tupac Amaru," a publication of the Universidad Nacional de Ingeniería, where he was studying.

At first, playing video games was an occasional pursuit; it was something he did rarely. Video games were expensive in Lima, and José Gabriel needed his money for books. However, the frequency of his visits to the video arcade gradually increased until eventually he was playing every day. From the beginning, he had shown a natural gift for video games. But as time progressed and he practiced more often, he became almost unbeatable.

Because he spent so much time playing video games, his grades dropped. Moreover, he forgot to eat and became thin. He even forgot to shave his face, which quickly gave him the appearance of a vagrant.

One day his best friend, Mario, entered the arcade. As soon as he saw José Gabriel, he went over to greet him. But José Gabriel was so absorbed in his game that he didn't hear his friend's voice. His eyes glowed with fascination as he concentrated his total attention on the game. He scored so many points that the machine stopped offering him free games. He became upset and kicked the machine violently. Then he walked out of the arcade.

The next day, José Gabriel had disappeared. Mario could not find him anywhere. He contacted his father, who called the police.

For three days, José Gabriel was missing. The police could not find him, and his father and Mario were afraid that he had been murdered.

EXERCISES

Prediction Exercises

Try to predict how the story ends. You may do group predictions in writing or individual predictions orally, but be ready to justify your predictions. After all predictions have been discussed, turn to the end of the story and read the ending. In making predictions, think about these questions:

1. Why did José Gabriel disappear?
2. What has happened to him?
3. Is he alive?
4. Will the police find him?

Comprehension Questions

These questions are related to the reading guide questions that preceded the story. Answer them and be ready to justify your answers when your teacher requests it.

1. Describe José Gabriel.
2. How does he change as a consequence of playing video games?
3. Does playing video games become a vice for him? Explain.
4. Why is he called a video game genius?
5. What irony occurs at the end of the story?

Questions for Further Discussion or Writing

The following questions are for discussion or writing. Choose one and answer it orally or write a brief response (5 to 10 sentences). You may wish to share written responses and discuss them.

1. Suppose there is a civic group that wishes to have all video games eliminated from your town. Would you support or oppose it? Why?
2. Have you ever had an interesting experience playing video games or observing other people playing? If so, describe your experience.
3. Do you like to play video games? Why or why not?

Optional Writing Exercise

Working in groups, write a short paragraph in which you explain the historical significance of the names José Gabriel and Tupac Amaru. (*Note*: The two names refer to the same historical figure.)

Obtaining Meaning from Context

If you do not recognize a word or expression based on its appearance, you may be able to *guess* its meaning based on context. Try to guess the meaning of the *italicized* expression. If possible, make your guess in English.

1. At first, playing video games was an occasional *pursuit*; it was something he did rarely.
2. But as time progressed and he practiced more often, he became almost *unbeatable*.
3. Because he spent so much time playing video games, his grades *dropped*.
4. He even forgot to shave his face, which quickly gave him the appearance of a *vagrant*.
5. As soon as he saw José Gabriel, he went over to *greet* him.
6. He became *upset* and kicked the machine violently.
7. For three days, José Gabriel was *missing*. The police could not find him. . . .
8. When he had finished, all the professors *rushed* over to talk to him.

STORY ENDING

After three days of searching, the Lima police reduced their efforts to find José Gabriel. The next day, José Gabriel reappeared at the university and presented a mathematical theory to the members of the faculty of the mathematics department. He also invited the faculty to accompany him to the video arcade.

It was an extraordinary sight—several distinguished professors in a video arcade. All the young people in the arcade stopped to observe this phenomenon. José Gabriel addressed the crowd briefly, then he proceeded to demonstrate his theory. At the end of fifteen minutes, he had defeated three video machines. This, he concluded, was one practical application of the mathematical theory he had developed. When he had finished, all the professors rushed over to talk to him. They wanted to offer him a special opportunity to lecture at the university. José Gabriel was dying of thirst. He walked over to a soda machine and deposited two coins. Then he pressed a button that said "Orange" and waited . . . and waited . . . and waited. . . .

CHAPTER 10

THE LONE SCUBA DIVER

Prereading

Discuss these questions before reading the story.

1. Is scuba diving popular in your country? If so, why do people like to go scuba diving?
2. Have you ever gone scuba diving? What experiences have you had?
3. What does the word *lone* mean? What is your opinion about a person going scuba diving alone?

Reading Guide Questions

Think about these questions while you read. Be prepared to answer them when you finish.

1. Why does Roberto go scuba diving alone?
2. What happens while he is scuba diving?

Roberto was a wonderful scuba diver. His favorite place to go diving was Luquillo because it was a very beautiful place and because he lived close by, in Rio Grande.

One Saturday morning, Roberto decided to go diving at Luquillo. He decided to invite his friend, Enrique, because Enrique liked scuba diving, too. Roberto called Enrique on the telephone. When Enrique answered, he told Roberto he could not go because he was helping his father to remount the engine of his car. Enrique suggested that Roberto invite José, another friend. When Roberto called José, José's mother answered the telephone. José was at a birthday party with Marta, and so he could not go scuba diving. Finally, Roberto decided to go scuba diving alone. He knew it was not a good idea, but he decided it would be O.K. just one time.

When he got to the beach, he parked his car carefully under a tree to protect it from the sun. After he parked his car, he removed all of his scuba diving equipment from his car. Then he put his equipment on. He put on his mask, his tank, and his flippers. Then he picked up his speargun and his underwater camera, and he was ready to dive.

Finally, he walked slowly into the water. When the water covered his stomach, he lay flat and began to swim on the surface. Then he began to go down in the water very slowly. When he was ten feet under the water, he stopped to adjust himself to the water pressure. He stayed at that level for awhile and took a few pictures with his camera. He was a very good photographer.

After awhile, Roberto began to move down again. He noticed that the water was darker, but he could still see well. He could see many different kinds of fish, plants, and rock formations. At twenty feet, he stopped again for several minutes to adjust to the increase in water pressure. During this time, he took some more pictures.

Roberto continued to move gradually down in the water. After some time, he reached the ocean floor. There he saw many beautiful things. He took pictures of everything with his camera. He took one picture of a starfish. He took another picture of a group of little fish that moved together like one big fish. He also took a picture of a piece of coral that looked like a giant hand with the fingers extended. Roberto was very happy about these pictures.

Suddenly, the water began to vibrate. It was an earth tremor. The force of the water pushed Roberto against the coral hand. His shoulder was cut by the coral, and he began to bleed. Roberto wanted to go up immediately, but he decided it was better to wait until the earth tremor stopped.

After a few seconds, the water stopped vibrating. Then Roberto started to go up. In the water, there was a cloud of blood. A long shadow streaked across the ocean floor toward Roberto. He saw the shadow. Then he saw the hammerhead shark. It was a killer shark, ten feet long. It was about thirty yards away and was moving toward him very fast. Roberto removed his air tank and held it in front of him with his hands. Then he descended toward the big coral hand on the ocean floor.

The shark was about ten yards away. Roberto could see its sharp teeth because its mouth was open. It wanted to eat him. Fortunately the giant coral hand protected Roberto, but he had only a thirty-minute air supply in his tank.

Then Roberto remembered his speargun. He gradually maneuvered it and aimed it at the shark. The shark was making circles around Roberto. He tried to hurt the shark with a spear, but the tank in his hands made shooting difficult. When he shot, the spear went over the shark. Roberto had one other spear. He loaded the speargun and tried again. This time the spear hit the shark, but only in the tail. Then Roberto knew he was going to die because in fifteen minutes he would have no air.

EXERCISES

Prediction Exercise

Try to predict how the story ends. Work in groups and write your prediction in a few sentences, or offer individual predictions orally. Be prepared to justify your prediction. After all of the predictions have been discussed, turn to the end of the chapter and read the story ending.

Comprehension Questions

These questions are related to the reading guide questions that preceded the story. When you answer them, be prepared to support your answers with information from the story when necessary.

1. Why did Roberto finally decide to go scuba diving alone?
2. Did he go down to the ocean floor rapidly or gradually? Explain.
3. What did he do while he was in the water?
4. How did he feel?
5. What happened that caused him to bleed?
6. What situation developed as a result of his bleeding?
7. How did Roberto protect himself?
8. Who helped Roberto and how?

Questions for Further Discussion or Writing

The following questions are for discussion or writing. Choose one and discuss it in class or answer it briefly in writing. You may wish to share your writing in class and discuss it.

1. Have you ever been alone in a situation where it was dangerous to be alone? Could the situation have been avoided? If so, how? What happened?
2. What situations are dangerous for a person who is alone and why? You may wish to choose one and write some examples.

3. If you have ever had an experience scuba diving, describe it. Were you alone or accompanied? Why was your experience interesting or exciting?

Optional Writing Exercise

Describe an animal that lives in the ocean or in rivers or lakes. Make your description concise (25 to 50 words). Where is the animal found (ocean, river, or lake)? Is it larger than a Volkswagen Beetle? What human characteristics do you associate with it (e.g., aggressiveness, cleanliness, shyness, intelligence, gracefulness, etc.)? What distinguishing characteristic does it have? Feel free to use your imaginations in writing this description. The other students can try to guess the name of the animal.

Obtaining Meaning from Context

If you do not recognize a word or expression based on its appearance, you may be able to *guess* its meaning based on context. Try to guess the meaning of the *italicized* expression. If possible, make your guess in English.

1. Then he put his equipment on. He put on his mask, his tank, and his *flippers*.
2. Then he picked up his speargun and his *underwater* camera, and he was ready to dive.
3. When he was ten feet under the water, he stopped to adjust himself to the water pressure. He stayed at that *level* for awhile. . . .
4. A long shadow *streaked* across the ocean floor toward Roberto.
5. He *loaded* the speargun and tried again.
6. He saw the hungry shark *closing in* to eat him.

STORY ENDING

In Rio Grande, Enrique and his father had finished mounting the car's engine. They were eating lunch when the earth began to tremble. Enrique decided to call Roberto to see if he had returned from the ocean. When he called, there was no answer, so he called José. José's mother told him that José was with Marta. Then Enrique knew that Roberto was alone under the water.

He and his father jumped into Enrique's car because his father's car, although normally faster, could not be driven fast with a recently reconstructed motor. Enrique drove as fast as possible toward Luquillo.

When they reached the beach, they found Roberto's car at their favorite spot. Then Enrique and his father put on their equipment, grabbed their spearguns, and went into the water.

Roberto's air was finished. He began to drop the tank because he had no strength. He saw the hungry shark closing in to eat him. Its mouth was open. Suddenly he saw an object hit the shark's head. Then another object pierced its side. This was the last thing he saw before he closed his eyes. He was not aware of Enrique and his father as they approached. They were loading their spearguns again, but it was not necessary because the shark was hurt. It swam away to find a safe place to recuperate.

Then Enrique went to Roberto and gave him some air from his tank. Roberto opened his eyes and smiled.

CHAPTER 11

WORKING TO LIVE

Prereading

Discuss the following questions before reading the story.

1. Why do people work? Are there different reasons? Explain.
2. If you could live in equal comfort by working or not working, which would you prefer? Why?

Reading Guide Questions

Think about this question while you read. Be prepared to answer the question after you finish.

1. Why does Mr. Vélez want to work?

Mr. Vélez was sixty-eight years old. When he was a young man, he had worked very hard. He had done farm work and he had been strong and happy.

Now Mr. Vélez was not happy because he had no work. He sat in a rocking chair and watched people and cars go by. Sometimes people would stop and talk to him for a few minutes, but most of the time Mr. Vélez was alone.

Mrs. Vélez was different. She was very busy. All day she worked in her house. She was happy because she was busy working. Mrs. Vélez kept her house very clean. She also cleaned the clothes, cooked the meals, watered the flowers, and washed the dishes every day.

One morning Mr. Vélez went for a walk. He walked quickly, not slowly. He seemed to have something very important to do. Finally he stopped at a little store and bought something.

At five o'clock in the afternoon, Mrs. Vélez called Mr. Vélez to supper. She called him three times, but he did not answer. Mrs. Vélez was annoyed because the food was getting cold. At five thirty, she called again. Again, Mr. Vélez did not answer.

At six o'clock, Mr. Vélez arrived home. He opened the gate with difficulty. When he reached the door, he fell to the floor. He was singing a song that he had invented. He had been drinking rum. When Mrs. Vélez saw him, she began to cry.

Mr. Vélez stood up with difficulty and walked to his room. He fell down three times, but he continued. He walked out of the house and into the street. In his hand, he was carrying a machete. He began cursing loudly and demonstrating, with the machete, how he would cut off the arms, legs, and head of anyone he disliked. First he moved the machete down very hard, then he quickly moved it horizontally. He repeated this process several times. When he was moving the machete downward for the third time, he accidentally cut a hole in one of his shoes. From the hole spurted red blood. When he saw the blood and felt the pain, Mr. Vélez fell to the concrete. He was unconscious.

At this time, two neighbors who were watching came to help Mr. Vélez out of the street. They were two strong, young men, and so they carried him into his house and put him in his bed.

The next afternoon, Mr. Vélez woke up in bed and was surprised to see his foot in a bandage. Mrs. Vélez had taken the unconscious Mr. Vélez to the emergency room for treatment. The doctor had bandaged his foot. But Mr. Vélez did not remember anything, so his wife described everything. Then he felt terrible because he remembered all the negative things he had said and how he had swung the machete in the air. When he remembered these things, he became angry and told his wife to leave him alone.

Three days later, Mr. Vélez tried to walk. He climbed slowly out of bed and limped out to the porch. He wanted to sit in his rocking chair, but he could not find it. When he asked his wife, she said that she had sold the chair to pay the doctor. Suddenly, he became very angry and stormed out of the house.

Mrs. Vélez was worried. She cried because she was afraid her husband might get drunk or even try to kill himself.

EXERCISES

Prediction Exercise

Try to predict how the story ends. Work in groups and write your prediction in a few sentences, or offer individual predictions orally. Be prepared to justify your prediction. After all predictions have been discussed, turn to the end of the chapter to read the story's ending. In making predictions, consider the following questions:

1. What do you think Mr. Vélez will do? Will he get drunk? Will he try to take his life?

2. How will the ending justify the title?

Comprehension Questions

These questions are related to the reading guide question that preceded the story. When you answer, be prepared to support your answer with information from the story.

1. At the beginning of the story, is Mr. Vélez happy? Give evidence.
2. What accident did he have and how did it occur?
3. Why did his wife sell his chair?
4. How did he react when he discovered she had sold his chair?
5. What did Mrs. Vélez and her children think had happened to Mr. Vélez?
6. What actually happened?
7. Why did Mr. Vélez want to work?

Questions for Further Discussion or Writing

Choose one question to discuss or write about. If you choose to write, you may also wish to read your paragraphs in class and discuss them.

1. Do you know people who are unemployed or retired? If so, how do they feel about the inactivity? Are they happy or not? Do they have hobbies or pastimes to keep them busy? How does unemployment or retirement affect them?
2. When you retire in the distant future, what kind of a life style do you want? Do you want to rest a lot? To keep busy? What conditions will make you happy when you are old and not permitted to work for an employer?

Optional Writing Exercise

If you do not like the ending of the story, rewrite it. In doing so, take into account the following questions: What happens to Mr. Vélez? Why is the story called "Working to Live"? Should the story end happily or could it end tragically?

Obtaining Meaning from Context

If you do not recognize a word or expression based on its appearance, you may be able to *guess* its meaning based on context. Try to guess the meaning of the *italicized* expression. If possible, make your guess in English.

1. Mrs. Vélez was *annoyed* because the food was getting cold.
2. He began *cursing* loudly and demonstrating, with the machete, how he would cut off the arms, legs, and head of anyone he disliked.
3. ... he accidentally cut a hole in one of his shoes. From the hole *spurted* red blood.
4. He climbed slowly out of bed and *limped* out to the porch.
5. Suddenly, he became very angry and *stormed* out of the house.

STORY ENDING

A week passed, and Mrs. Vélez did not see her husband. She had called the police, but they had no information about Mr. Vélez. She was convinced that her husband was dead. She called her children on the telephone and they all came to the house in Caguas. Manuel came from Cidra, Teresa from Humacao, Luis from Las Piedras, and Sara from Caguas Norte to talk to their mother, to console her, and to prepare for a funeral.

On Sunday, all the family and all of Mr. Vélez's friends were in the church to pray for his spirit. The priest was praying out loud.

Suddenly, Mr. Vélez walked into the church. At first, nobody saw him. Then his wife looked up and screamed. She fell to the floor unconcious. She believed that it was Mr. Vélez's spirit that she saw. Some people tried to help her, while others went over to Mr. Vélez to learn where he had been.

When his wife sold his rocking chair, he had become angry. He had not known what to do. He began walking, and as he was walking he got an idea. He would look for a job. He thought about the employment office, but they would not help him because of his age.

But he did not stop trying. He had a friend with a farm in Juncos, and he decided to ask the friend for work. He took a bus to the plaza, and from there he walked to his friend's farm. When his friend saw him walking on a bloody foot, he asked why Mr. Vélez had walked such a great distance on a bloody foot. Then Mr. Vélez explained his situation. His friend smiled and immediately offered him a job. Mr. Vélez had been working in Juncos all week.

Now Mr. Vélez was happy because he was working. When his wife opened her eyes, he explained everything. Then the two old people were both happy.

CHAPTER 12

THE COSTLY DECISION

Prereading

Discuss the following questions before reading the story.

1. Why do people get married?
2. What are some good reasons? What are some bad ones?

Reading Guide Questions

Think about these questions while you read. Be ready to answer them after you finish.

1. Why does Maritza get married?
2. Why is the story called "The Costly Decision"?

Maritza and Armando attended the same high school and they were friends. Armando was a responsible, serious student who always treated Maritza with respect and generosity. She admired his mature nature and gave him support in difficult situations. However, they seldom saw each other except at school.

The reason for this was that Maritza's parents were very strict with her. They would not let her go out with friends because they were afraid she would get involved with a boy and become pregnant.

As time passed, Maritza became increasingly frustrated by her situation. She wanted to have an active, normal social life. She wanted to have fun with her friends. But her parents continued to be very strict and authoritarian with her. Maritza became introverted. She began to read romantic novels in her bedroom with the door closed. She fantasized about the men in these novels. She hoped that a man would come to rescue her by taking her from her parents' home.

More than a year passed, and Armando graduated. He found a job as a teller in a bank and continued studying at night and on weekends to complete his associate's degree. Maritza, who was two years younger, continued high school. The situation in her home remained the same.

One day Maritza went to her father to ask permission to go to a dance at the high school. She explained that there would be teachers at the dance and good supervision, but her father said no. She tried to continue the conversation, but he was watching his favorite detective program and ordered her to be quiet.

She decided to escape. She went to the bank where Armando worked and told him she wanted to talk. After the bank closed, they went to a small restaurant and Maritza asked Armando to marry her. He was overjoyed because he had always secretly loved Maritza, and of course he said yes.

They got married, rented an apartment, and began to live together as husband and wife. During the first few months, they were happy. They went to the theater and dancing, and they enjoyed the conjugal bliss of the marriage bed. Maritza thought that she was in heaven.

EXERCISES

Prediction Exercise

Try to predict how the story ends. You may work in groups and write your prediction in a few sentences or offer individual predictions orally. Be prepared to justify your prediction. After all predictions have been discussed, turn to the end of the chapter and read the story's ending. In making predictions, keep in mind the title of the story.

Comprehension Questions

These questions are related to the reading guide questions. When you answer, be ready to support your answer with information from the story if necessary.

1. Does Armando love Maritza?
2. How do Maritza's parents treat her?
3. Describe her father's behavior.
4. Is Maritza happy in her parents' home?
5. Does she love Armando?
6. Why does she get married?
7. Is the marriage a happy one at first? Why or why not?
8. After the first few months, what change occurs in the marriage?
9. What conflicts exist between Maritza and Armando?
10. How does the story end? Is it a happy ending?

Questions for Further Discussion or Writing

Choose one question. Discuss it in class or write a brief, one-paragraph answer (approximately 5 to 10 sentences). You may wish to share your paragraphs by reading and discussing them.

1. Do you know anyone who got married under pressure? If so, why did the person get married? Is he or she happy today, in your opinion?
2. What steps do you think two people should take before they get married? Explain.
3. What circumstances in Maritza's home created pressure for her to get married? If you had been her mother or father, how would you have acted differently?

Optional Writing Exercise

Give this story a new title. In doing so, consider these questions: Why did Maritza get married? Why did her first marriage fail? Why did she get married again instead of returning home?

Obtaining Meaning from Context

If you do not recognize a word or expression based on its appearance, you may be able to *guess* its meaning based on context. Try to guess the meaning of the *italicized* expression. If possible, make your guess in English.

1. . . . they were afraid she would get involved with a boy and become *pregnant*.
2. She fantasized about the men in these novels. She hoped that a man would come to *rescue* her by taking her from her parents' home.
3. He was *overjoyed* because he had always secretly loved Maritza, and of course he said yes.
4. They went to the theater and dancing, and they enjoyed the *conjugal bliss* of the marriage bed.
5. Maritza thought that she was in *heaven*.

STORY ENDING

However, tensions soon developed in their marriage. Maritza wanted to spend all the time dancing and having fun, while Armando insisted that it was necessary for him to spend time studying. He wanted Maritza to finish high school, but she was opposed to this idea. In addition, Armando was interested in forming a family soon, but Maritza was not. She wanted to be free to go dancing and to parties. During the next year, Armando continued studying. While he was in school, Maritza went out secretly. She met another man and became romantically involved. When Armando discovered this situation, he requested a divorce. Maritza granted the divorce and married the other man, but he abused her and went out with other women. Maritza was never happy.

CHAPTER 13

THE GOOD SAMARITANS

Prereading

Discuss the following questions before reading the story.

1. What is a good Samaritan?
2. Have you ever acted as a good Samaritan or received the help of a good Samaritan? Explain.

Reading Guide Questions

Think about these questions while you read. Be ready to answer them when you finish.

1. Who are the good Samaritans in this story and what do they do?
2. Who do the good Samaritans help? Why does (do) the person(s) need help?

Julia and Manuel were teenagers. They were going steady. In other words, they had a serious relationship and were contemplating spending the future together. They typically spent their weekends together going to the beach or to a movie. Teatro Caguas was near Julia's house; consequently, she and Manuel usually walked to the theater. But they always took an indirect route to avoid passing the public housing project. Public housing projects do not generally have good reputations, and Julia and Manuel thought that people who lived in such places were bad.

One Saturday evening, Julia and Manuel decided to see a movie. They took their usual route to the theater and enjoyed a long, pleasant walk together. It gave them the opportunity to develop a romantic mood and to dream about the future.

The movie ended at 9:00 p.m., so when they left the theater it was dark. Because of their romantic mood, the two young people did not notice a car parked on the corner in front of the theater. In the car, three men were drinking whiskey. The men began to follow the young couple. Then they pulled up alongside Julia and Manuel and said something vulgar. When Manuel responded to their vulgarity by calling them idiots, the car stopped and the men started to get out. Julia grabbed Manuel by the hand and pulled him frantically. Initially, he wanted to stay to fight with the men, but then he thought of the danger for Julia and followed her. The two teenagers changed directions and ran desperately. The three men got in their car and followed.

Unconsciously, Julia had taken the route that went by the public housing project, probably because it was the shortest way to her parents' house. Suddenly, the car that was pursuing them increased speed and disappeared. Julia and Manuel felt relieved. They stopped running and started to walk, but then they noticed that they were in front of the housing project. This made them nervous again. All at once, their thoughts were interrupted by the noise of car doors slamming. Then, in front of them, they saw the three men who had been following them. They had no alternative, so they ran inside one of the apartment buildings of the project.

EXERCISES

Prediction Exercise

Try to predict how the story ends. Work in groups and write your prediction in a few sentences, or offer individual predictions orally. Be prepared to justify your prediction. After all predictions have been discussed, turn to the end of the chapter to read the story's ending. In making predictions, think about these questions:

1. What will happen next?
2. Will the men enter the apartment building? Will they discover Julia and Manuel?
3. How will the ending of the story justify the title?
4. Will the experience affect Julia and Manuel's attitude toward public housing projects?

Comprehension Questions

These questions are related to the reading guide questions that preceded the story. Answer them and be prepared to justify your answer if your teacher requests it.

1. Where do Manuel and Julia go on Saturday?
2. Why do they take an indirect route?

3. What dangerous situation develops when they are returning home?
4. Who is Mrs. Sanchez and how does she help the young couple?
5. Describe Mrs. Sanchez's apartment. Describe her treatment of Julia and Manuel.
6. Describe Rogelio. How does he help Julia and Manuel?
7. Do you think Mrs. Sanchez and Rogelio influence Julia and Manuel's attitude toward people who live in public housing projects? Why or why not?

Questions for Further Discussion or Writing

Choose one question and discuss it in class or write a brief, one-paragraph answer (approximately 5 to 10 sentences). You may wish to read your paragraphs in class and discuss them, too.

1. What stereotype do Julia and Manuel believe? What other stereotypes exist (e.g., concerning the rich, children, old people, women, etc.)? To what extent are these stereotypes true? (*Note:* For writing, choose one stereotype and treat it in depth.)
2. Give examples of good Samaritans from earlier stories. Discuss them.

Optional Writing Exercise

Give this story a new title. Keep in mind the help provided by Mrs. Sanchez and Rogelio and the attitude of Julia and Manuel toward people in public housing projects. Be ready to defend your title.

Obtaining Meaning from Context

If you do not recognize a word or expression based on its appearance, you may be able to *guess* its meaning based on context. Try to guess the meaning of the *italicized* expression. If possible, make your guess in English.

1. They typically *spent* their weekends together going to the beach or to a movie.
2. It gave them the opportunity to develop a romantic *mood* and to dream about the future.

3. Julia grabbed Manuel by the hand and pulled him *frantically*.
4. All at once, their thoughts were interrupted by the noise of car doors *slamming*.
5. Mrs. Sanchez went into the kitchen; meanwhile, Julia and Manuel examined the unfamiliar *surroundings*.
6. The coffee cups were *chipped* and the flowers painted on the cups were *faded*, but the coffee was delicious.
7. Mrs. Sanchez sat on a *rickety* wooden chair in front of Julia and Manuel and smiled at them.

STORY ENDING

The two young people were terrified. They had no escape. Then, unexpectedly, a voice called to them and they saw the hand of a woman signalling them to follow. They obeyed. They followed the woman upstairs and into her apartment on the second floor.

When they were safely inside, the woman locked the door and turned off the lights. In a minute, the three men walked through the hall. They were talking to each other angrily. They stopped in front of the woman's apartment to listen, but everything was quiet. Then they said some bad words, and one man threw a bottle against the wall. The noise was so frightening that Julia almost screamed. However, after a few moments, the men returned to their car and drove away.

When the men had gone, the woman turned on the lights. Julia and Manuel released deep sighs of relief. Then the woman introduced herself. Her name was Mrs. Sanchez. She invited the couple to sit down. They observed that the sofa was deteriorated, but when they sat down, it felt comfortable. Mrs. Sanchez went into the kitchen; meanwhile, Julia and Manuel examined their unfamiliar surroundings. There was no carpet on the floor, but the bare floor looked very clean. The windows had no curtains. On the walls, the only adornments were an old picture of a bride and groom and a crucifix. When Mrs. Sanchez returned from the kitchen, she brought a tray with coffee, crackers, cheese, and guava paste. The coffee cups were chipped and the flowers painted on the cups were faded, but the coffee was delicious. Mrs. Sanchez sat on a rickety wooden chair in front of Julia and Manuel and smiled at them.

Suddenly there was a knock at the door. Julia and Manuel immediately tensed, but Mrs. Sanchez smiled with recognition. She went to the door and opened it, and in stepped a powerfully built young man. Mrs. Sanchez introduced him as Rogelio, and this is when Julia and Manuel finally offered their names. Rogelio sat down on the floor and Mrs. Sanchez brought him a cup of coffee. A conversation developed, and Julia and Manuel learned that Rogelio had a protective attitude toward Mrs. Sanchez. He checked on her every day and whenever there was potential danger. In a minute, another knock was heard. This time, Rogelio went to the door and let in Mr. Suarez, who lived across the hall. Mr. Suarez walked with the assistance of a cane, but he also carried a pistol that he was very adept at using. He had used it on various occasions to frighten would-be assailants. Soon, everyone was conversing animatedly and sharing interesting stories.

When the coffee and food were finished, Mrs. Sanchez collected the cups on the tray and returned them to the kitchen. Then she asked Rogelio to escort Julia and Manuel to their home. She invited them to return to visit her another day. They thanked her for her hospitality.

When they reached Julia's house, they told Rogelio how grateful they were for his help. Then they said good-bye and went inside to tell Julia's parents about their scary but educational experience.

CHAPTER 14

THE HABIT

Prereading

Discuss these questions before reading the story.

1. What is a habit?
2. Are habits easy to change?
3. Describe a bad habit and explain why you think it would be easy or difficult to change.

Reading Guide Questions

Think about these questions while you read. Be ready to answer them when you finish.

1. What habit does the old man have?
2. During the course of the story, does he change this habit?

In the town of Parral, Mexico, an old man sat in front of a cafeteria. His clothes were dirty and his face was covered with short, white hairs. His eyes were filled with red lines that looked like tiny rivers running in many directions. His shoes and hat were full of holes. He held his hat in front of him. When people passed, he asked for anything they could give him. He began collecting money at eight o'clock in the morning, but at twelve o'clock, he still had only a little change in his hat. He needed almost twice as much to buy something to drink.

At three o'clock in the afternoon, the old man counted his money again. Now he had almost enough. He still needed more, but maybe he could persuade González to sell him a bottle. With this idea in mind, he stood up and walked toward González's little store.

When he arrived, the old man went to the back of the store and took a flask of rum from the shelf. He knew the price, but he placed the flask on the counter and asked González if he had enough money. The old man placed the change on the counter, and González counted it. After he counted the change one time, González looked at the old man. The old man's condition made González feel sorry for him. He counted the money again and said there was enough.

The old man was walking along the road at night. It was dark except for the lights of passing cars. He was standing at an intersection.

He held the flask of rum above his mouth and poured the last few drops down his throat. Then he threw the empty flask into the grass beside the road and started to cross the street. He thought the cars were crawling and that he was walking fast. The opposite was true. When he reached the middle of the road, his legs began to wobble and he fell down. At that moment, a car came speeding toward him. He saw the wheels approaching his head, and then he lost consciousness.

When he awoke, two boys about the age of his grandson stood over him. He was beside the road in the grass. It was their car that had almost hit him, but they had seen him just in time and stopped to help. One of the boys asked if he was all right. He said he was O.K. The other boy asked him where he lived. He said only that he lived in town, because he did not want them to know exactly where he lived. The second boy asked him in what part of town he lived. He said the name of a street and they said they would take him there.

Then the two boys helped the old man stand up and get into the car. When they reached the street, the old man thanked them and got out. They said they would take him to his home, but he said he was going to meet a friend first. Then they said good-bye and drove away.

EXERCISES

Prediction Exercise

Try to predict how the story ends. Work in groups and write your prediction in a few sentences, or offer individual predictions orally. Be prepared to justify your prediction. After all predictions are discussed, turn to the end of the chapter and read the ending. In making predictions, keep in mind the title.

Comprehension Questions

These questions are related to the reading guide questions that preceded the story. Answer these questions and be prepared to justify or explain your answers based on information from the story

1. How does the old man obtain money?
2. How does he use the money?
3. In your opinion, does González help the old man? Explain.

4. How does the old man almost get killed?
5. How do we know the old man has a drinking habit?
6. Do you think he will ever change?

Questions for Further Discussion or Writing

Choose one question and discuss it in class or write a brief, one-paragraph answer (approximately 5 to 10 sentences). You may wish to read your paragraphs in class and discuss them.

1. Why do people become alcoholics? What can be done to help them?
2. Name some other bad habits (e.g., overeating, smoking, etc.). How do they affect life? (*Note:* For writing, choose one bad habit.)
3. Have you ever known an alcoholic? If so, discuss how his or her life is or was affected by alcoholism.

Optional Writing Exercise

Describe the consequences of a particular bad habit but do not mention the habit. The other people in the class will try to guess the habit. Do your writing in groups and make your description brief (3 or 4 sentences). You might think about these questions when you write your description: Does this habit affect one's appearance? Does it affect health? Behavior?

Obtaining Meaning from Context

If you do not recognize a word or expression based on its appearance, you may be able to *guess* its meaning based on context. Try to guess the meaning of the *italicized* expression. If possible, make your guess in English.

1. When he arrived, the old man went to the back of the store and took a *flask* of rum from the shelf.
2. The old man's condition made González *feel sorry* for him.
3. He counted the money a second time and said there was *enough*.

4. He held the flask of rum above his mouth and poured the last few drops down his *throat*.
5. He thought the cars were *crawling* and that he was walking fast.
6. When he reached the middle of the road, his legs began to *wobble* and he fell down.

STORY ENDING

At eight o'clock the next morning, the old man was sitting before the cafeteria with his hat in his hands, asking for money.

CHAPTER 15

THE UGLY SUITOR

Prereading

Discuss these questions before reading the story.

1. What qualities do you consider important in a member of the opposite sex and why?
2. Would you marry a person who was physically unattractive? Why or why not?

Reading Guide Questions

Think about these questions while you read. Be ready to answer them when you finish.

1. How does the ugly suitor try to attract the attention of the beautiful girl, Marisol?
2. What qualities does the ugly suitor have?

Marisol was a beautiful girl. She studied at the Universidad de Valle in Cali, Colombia.

A young man named Jesus attended the same school. He was an average student, but he liked natural science. His favorite class was biology because it is the study of life. Although he needed his time to study, he also spent four hours a week doing volunteer work with handicapped students. On weekends, Jesus worked part-time to help his parents. However, despite his good qualities, Jesus was not popular with the girls. He was physically weak and unattractive. He wore thick glasses because he was nearsighted, and his arms and legs were as thin and unmuscular as spaghetti.

He was in love with Marisol. He thought that she was beautiful and he wanted to know her better. But he could not get close to her. Every time he saw her, she was with some other young man. Jesus was shy with girls and he was afraid that Marisol would reject him.

The first time that he tried to approach Marisol, she was with a big fellow with muscular arms who was an athlete. They were at the university swimming pool. Jesus had an idea that might help him attract Marisol's attention. He went to the high diving board and stood at the end. Suddenly everyone was quiet because they were looking at Jesus.

82 The Ugly Suitor

Marisol and the athlete were looking too. Then Jesus tried to make a spectacular dive, but he slipped and fell into the water. Everyone thought that he was trying to be funny. They laughed and paid no more attention to him.

Another time, they were in biology class. The professor had asked a question and nobody could answer it. Jesus looked at Marisol and smiled, but she did not smile back. He raised his hand, and, when the professor called on him, Jesus gave an impressive answer. He was happy until he looked at Marisol and discovered that she was talking to another boy.

Finally Jesus decided to do something that was emotionally risky.

EXERCISES

Prediction Exercise

Try to predict how the story ends. Work in groups and write your predictions in a few sentences, or offer individual predictions orally. Be prepared to justify your prediction. After all predictions have been discussed, turn to the end of the chapter and read the story's ending. In making predictions, take into consideration the following questions:

1. What will Jesus do? (Remember that it is emotionally risky.)
2. Will Marisol ever give him an opportunity to know her better? Why or why not?

Comprehension Questions

These questions are related to the reading guide questions that preceded the story. When you answer them, be ready to support your answers with information from the story if your teacher requests it.

1. Describe Marisol.
2. Describe Jesus. What is he like as a person? Physically?
3. How does he try to impress Marisol at the swimming pool and how does she react?
4. How does he try to get her attention in biology class and how does she react?

5. What is the last thing he does to get her attention and how does she react?

Questions for Further Discussion or Writing

Choose one question and discuss it in class or write a brief, one-paragraph response (approximately 5 to 10 sentences). If you write a paragraph, you may wish to read it in class and discuss it.

1. If you were Marisol, would you give Jesus an opportunity? Suppose the situation were reversed. Would you give the girl an opportunity?
2. What qualities do you consider important in a member of the opposite sex? Describe your ideal spouse.

Optional Writing Exercise

Rewrite the ending. In doing so, think about these questions: How would you change Jesus's behavior? Marisol's actions? Would you alter the role of the muscular fellow? If so, how?

Obtaining Meaning from Context

If you do not recognize a word or expression based on its appearance, you may be able to *guess* its meaning based on context. Try to guess the meaning of the *italicized* expression. If possible, make your guess in English.

1. Although he needed his time to study, he also spent four hours a week doing volunteer work with *handicapped* students.
2. He wore thick glasses because he was *nearsighted*, and his arms and legs were as thin and unmuscular as spaghetti.
3. Jesus was *shy* with girls and he was afraid that Marisol would reject him.
4. Then Jesus tried to make a spectacular *dive*, but he slipped and fell into the water.
5. When he finished the poem, Jesus signed his name and put it in an *envelope* with Marisol's name on it.

6. The athlete laughed and made an *unkind* remark about Jesus's physical appearance.

STORY ENDING

He decided to write a love poem and give it to Marisol. He spent several hours thinking of something special and finally he came up with this:

> You my beauty are
> who laugh with such spontaneity
> who give life to me by existing
> who do not know that I exist.
> You my beauty are
> who with one smile could give eternal happiness
> who with a "yes" could grant my dreams
> who with a touch could produce my felicity
> who only look the other way.
> Come my beauty and stop the chase.
> Others may offer you superficial things.
> But only I offer you love.

When he finished the poem, Jesus signed his name and put it in an envelope with Marisol's name on it. The next day, he secretly put the envelope in Marisol's biology book.

The following day, when Jesus saw Marisol, she smiled. Jesus thought that she was laughing at him. He felt ashamed and ran. He ran fast, but soon he became tired because of his asthma and Marisol caught up with him. She put her hand on his arm and smiled. She told him thank you for the poem.

At that moment, her muscular friend, the athlete, came up. He put his hand around Marisol's arm and told her to come with him, but Marisol said no. She wanted to stay with Jesus. The athlete laughed and made an unkind remark about Jesus's physical appearance. Marisol defended Jesus. She said that he was a beautiful, sensitive human being. Then she gave him a kiss. The athlete walked away very angry, and Jesus and Marisol sat down under a tree to talk.

CHAPTER 16

SARA

Prereading

Discuss these questions before reading the story.

1. How would you like to spend your old age? In other words, what would be an ideal old age for you?
2. How many old people in the present society of your country are happy about the way they are spending their old age?

Reading Guide Questions

Think about these questions while you read. Be ready to answer them when you finish.

1. What kind of person is Sara at the beginning of the story?
2. What change occurs in her and why?

Sara was seventy years old. She was slender and straight like a pine tree, despite her years, and she moved with grace. Her hair was gray, but it had streaks of black in it which made her look like a vigorous person. She wore colorful clothing and tried very hard to look attractive in a mature fashion. Her eyes were quite intense. Their color was green, like emeralds. She seemed to see great distances with them. Her mind was also very keen. She could remember events that had occurred many years ago and she could argue as logically as anyone. Some people said she should have been a lawyer because her mind and memory were keen. Sara was also a very active person, and very charitable. She visited hospitals to talk to the sick people. She donated her blood for use in the hospitals. She tried to help the poor people, especially people who needed food. Often she walked to places in the country where there were starving children. She would bring big loaves of bread and chunks of cheese for them to eat. She was happy to see their faces light up with hope.

Sara lived with her grandchildren because her children were all dead. One of her sons had died in an airplane accident. Another had become ill during a trip into the Amazon. Her daughter had been a missionary worker and had been murdered by a jealous native woman in Africa.

Sara's grandchildren were young. They were in their twenties. Her granddaughter's husband was an architect and very wealthy. They lived in a wonderful house with plenty of space and very comfortable facilities.

The architect, Marcelo Collazo, was a very busy man. He was almost never in the house to spend time with the children. Sara's granddaughter, Pilar, was not employed. However, she was quite occupied, too, because she was involved with many social activities. Neither Pilar nor Marcelo spent much time in the house with Sara and the children. There was a nurse who cared for the children most of the time.

One day Sara became ill. It was merely a cold and it did not last more than five days, but Marcelo was visibly disturbed. He thought that Sara was very old. He expected her to become a serious problem in the future because of her age. He thought that she might require attention. As a result, Marcelo decided to have Sara put in a nursing home for the aged. This would cost money, but it would be easy. Having her at home would be inconvenient.

Pilar initially protested Marcelo's decision, but soon she accepted it. She was very busy socially and did not have time to take care of her grandmother if the old woman got sick.

Marcelo was planning to reveal his decision to Sara, but Sara accidentally overheard a conversation between Pilar and Marcelo and discovered his plans. When she learned that they planned to put her in a nursing home, she decided to try to stop them. She was a vigorous, healthy woman with lots of energy and she did not want to be put in a nursing home.

To demonstrate how healthy and strong she was, the next day Sara got up early and prepared breakfast for Marcelo and Pilar. She took it to their bedroom as a surprise. It was a delicious breakfast and they enjoyed it; however, Marcelo demonstrated no intention of altering his decision.

When this idea did not have positive results, Sara decided to replace the nurse who was caring for the children. She found the nurse a job working in another home and started caring for the children herself. She thought maybe this would convince Marcelo because it would save him money. The children were very happy because their great-grandmother loved them and gave them special attention that the nurse never gave them. However, when Marcelo discovered what Sara had done, he showed violent opposition.

Soon Marcelo hired another nurse to care for the children. When this happened, Sara decided to occupy herself by cleaning the house.

She knew that the appearance of the house was very important to Marcelo and Pilar. However, she discovered that the house was immaculate. There was a maid who came twice a week and did an excellent job of keeping the house clean.

By this time, Sara was very unhappy. She had neglected the poor people in the fields, but her efforts to impress Marcelo were failures. What could she do to avoid being placed in a nursing home?

Then she had an idea. She decided to escape! She would hide in the country with the poor people. They would help her because they loved her. She secretly prepared for her escape. She prepared a small bag of clothing and other necessary things. Then she waited for the night. When night came, she slipped out of bed silently and went to the children's room. She kissed each child gently on the forehead and then she left.

Unfortunately, the police discovered her before she could reach her destination and they returned her to her grandchildren's house.

The next day Marcelo took Sara to the nursing home. She struggled physically in a last effort to avoid going, but it was inevitable.

When they reached the nursing home, Sara saw other old people sitting passively watching TV or being attended by nurses. They acted like vegetables! One old man who looked perfectly normal physically was receiving assistance from a nurse in moving from his bed to his chair. Sara closed her eyes.

After some months, Marcelo and Pilar finally decided to visit Sara in the nursing home. They wore their best clothing so they would look nice. The children were excited because they loved their great-grandmother and missed her very much.

EXERCISES

Prediction Exercise

Try to predict how the story ends. Work in groups and write your prediction in a few sentences, or offer individual predictions orally. Be prepared to justify your prediction. After all predictions are discussed, turn to the end of the chapter and read the ending. In making predictions, consider the following questions:

1. What will happen when Marcelo, Pilar, and the children visit Sara? Will Sara be happy to see them?

2. Will Marcelo change his mind and offer to take Sara back?
3. Will Sara be happy in the nursing home?

Comprehension Questions

These questions are related to the reading guide questions that preceded the story. Answer these questions and be prepared to justify or explain your answers based on information from the story.

1. Describe Sara.
2. What kinds of things does she do to help people?
3. Describe Sara's grandchildren.
4. What decision does Marcelo make concerning Sara?
5. What does Sara do to try to change Marcelo's decision?
6. Does Marcelo change his decision?
7. Why does Sara try to go to the country?
8. Describe how Sara changes.

Questions for Further Discussion or Writing

Choose one paragraph and discuss it in class or write a brief, one-paragraph response (5 to 10 sentences). If you write, you may wish to read your paragraphs and discuss them.

1. Is this story realistic? Explain.
2. Have you ever known anyone like Sara? If so, tell the class about that person.
3. If you could change the way old people are treated in your country, what would you change? If you think that no change is necessary, give evidence to support this view.

Optional Writing Exercise

Give the story a new title. Explain in a short paragraph why the new title is better than the original.

Obtaining Meaning from Context

If you do not recognize a word or expression based on its appearance, you may be able to *guess* its meaning based on context. Try to guess the meaning of the *italicized* expression. If possible, make your guess in English.

1. She was *slender* and straight like a pine tree, despite her years, and she moved with grace.
2. Her mind was also very *keen*. She could remember events that had occurred many years ago and she could argue as logically as anyone.
3. Often she walked to places in the country where there were *starving* children. She would bring big loaves of bread and chunks of cheese for them to eat.
4. Soon Marcelo *hired* another nurse to care for the children.
5. When night came, she *slipped* out of her bed silently and went to the children's room.
6. When the woman looked up, her eyes were *dull* and cloudy.

STORY ENDING

The family finally arrived at the nursing home and asked one of the nurses to direct them to Sara's room. The nurse asked them to follow her and soon they arrived at Sara's room. On the edge of the bed was an old woman. She looked ninety years old. Her hair was gray with a yellow tinge. She was bent over like a tree that has too much fruit. She was wearing a shawl to protect her from the cold, although the temperature in the room was not cold. When the woman looked up, her eyes were dull and cloudy. It was hard to believe that this old woman was Sara. She seemed like a different person. She was very passive and lethargic. The children went to her and embraced her. They smiled and said they loved her, but Sara did not recognize them. She pointed to the television set in the corner of the room. There was a family on the screen. "That is my family," she said, smiling. Then she fell asleep.

CHAPTER 17

THE DEATH OF
THE MANGO TREE

Prereading

Discuss the following questions before reading the story.

1. What do you value in life? Place the following items in order, beginning with the item you value most: time with your family, convenience, love, a new car, money, pleasant working conditions, fame, nice clothes, friendship.
2. What things that are not on this list do you consider important? What things that are on the list do you consider of little importance?

Reading Guide Questions

Think about these questions while you read. Be prepared to answer them when you finish.

1. Why is the mango tree destroyed?
2. What does it symbolize?

Amelia Amalbert was a beautiful old woman who lived in a small, pretty house. Amelia was sixty-two years old. She received a very adequate sum of money from the Veterans Administration because her husband, who was a soldier during World War II, had died in battle. However, even though Amelia's husband was dead, she was happy because she felt that the spirit of her husband was always with her in her little house, especially when she was in the yard behind her house. She tried to make some improvements in the house every year so that it would look nice. In fact, the appearance of her house became an obsession.

One year she decided to add a concrete patio and aluminum roof to her back yard. Besides being an attractive addition to the house, this would be a cool, comfortable place to sit in her rocking chair and think about the times when her husband was still alive.

Amelia hired two men to put up the roof and lay down the floor. They came one day and took measurements so they would know how much material they needed. The next day they brought the materials and began to put up the roof. In two days, they finished putting up the roof, but the concrete floor took longer because the concrete had to dry and harden. Finally, after one week, the work was finished. Then Amelia paid the men for their labor. When the two men had left, she went to the front porch for her rocking chair. She took the chair to the new patio and sat in the cool shade provided by the aluminum roof. There she sat and rocked, happy because she finally had a comfortable place to sit and think about her husband and to be close to his spirit. Soon Amelia was asleep. She dreamed of her husband, Rodrigo, and she was content. In her dream, Rodrigo was young and handsome.

For several months, Amelia enjoyed her new patio. It was pleasant and she knew that the spirit of her husband was happy. Then one day a neighbor came by. The neighbor was admiring Amelia's new patio. She said it was nice and that it looked comfortable. But when she noticed the mango tree in Amelia's back yard, the expression on her face changed. Suddenly she was not smiling. She told Amelia that it was necessary to cut down the mango tree—to eliminate it. Amelia was surprised. She did not understand why she should cut down the mango tree. Rodrigo had planted the tree many years ago and he had always treated it as something special. She knew that he would not have wanted her to eliminate it. But the neighbor explained why it was necessary to cut down the tree. She said that the roots would grow and cause the concrete to crack. Eventually, the floor would be full of cracks.

Now this made Amelia unhappy. She did not want her patio to be full of cracks, especially since she was planning to cover it with decorative tiles. The decorative tiles would look terrible if they were cracked. She decided to hire a man to cut down the mango tree. She called a man who specialized in this kind of work, and he promised to come the next day.

At eight o'clock the next morning, somebody knocked loudly on the front door. The noise startled Amelia, and she immediately got up to see who it was. It was Mr. Aponte, the man who was supposed to cut down the mango tree. Amelia showed Mr. Aponte to the back yard and told him to call her when he finished.

About half an hour passed. Amelia had fallen asleep, but now suddenly she woke up. Outside, she could hear Mr. Aponte chopping at the mango tree, but that was not what made her wake up. She had heard some other sound that was very strange and very sad. When Mr. Aponte hit the tree with the hatchet, she heard the sound again. To Amelia, it sounded like the voice of her beloved Rodrigo, and he seemed to be suffering greatly. But why was Rodrigo suffering?

Then, in a moment, Amelia knew the answer. Every time the hatchet hit the tree, her dead husband moaned sorrowfully. Every chop with the hatchet seemed to cut deeper into Rodrigo's soul. Amelia was terrified. She ran outside. When she reached the back yard, Mr. Aponte was smiling and the mango tree was lying on the ground. Now the sound of her husband's voice stopped. Amelia knew that her husband's spirit had been inside the mango tree. Now his spirit was gone and Amelia was alone.

EXERCISES

Comprehension Questions

These questions are related to the reading guide questions that preceded the story. In answering them, be prepared to justify your answers with information from the story.

1. Why was Amelia happy at the beginning of the story?
2. What was her obsession?
3. What did she have constructed in her back yard?
4. What recommendation did her neighbor make? Why?
5. Why was the ending of the story sad? What was the significance of the mango tree? When did Amelia discover its significance?

Questions for Further Discussion or Writing

Choose one question and discuss it in class or write a paragraph in response. If you write a paragraph, you may wish to read and discuss it in class.

1. What does the death of the mango tree signify in terms of human values?
2. Have you ever, consciously or unconsciously, chosen something material over something spiritual? If so, explain. What did you choose and why? How did you feel afterward? Were there benefits to your decision? Were there disadvantages or regrets?

Optional Writing Exercise

Give this story a new title and justify your choice in a brief paragraph.

Obtaining Meaning from Context

If you do not recognize a word or expression based on its appearance, you may be able to *guess* its meaning based on context. Try to guess the meaning of the *italicized* expression. If possible, make your guess in English.

1. She tried to make some *improvements* in the house every year so that it would look nice.
2. Rodrigo had *planted* the tree many years ago and he had always treated it as something special.
3. Outside, she could hear Mr. Aponte *chopping* at the mango tree.
4. Every time the hatchet hit the tree, her dead husband *moaned sorrowfully*.

Cloze Exercise

Do this exercise in class unless otherwise instructed. You may work individually or in groups, but do not consult the original text for answers. When you finish, your teacher will have you check your answers. It is not necessary for your answers to be the same as those in the story, but they should be logical. When your answers differ from those in the story, discuss why they are or are not logical. *Note:* This exercise is not intended as a test or graded assignment.

  Amelia Amalbert was a beautiful _____ woman who lived in a _____, pretty house. Amelia was sixty-two _____ old. She received a very _____ sum of money from the _____ Administration because her husband, who _____ a soldier during World War _____, had died in battle. However, _____ though Amelia's husband was dead, _____ was happy because she felt _____ the spirit of her husband _____ always with her in her _____ house, especially when she was _____ the yard behind her house. _____ tried to make some improvements _____ the house every year so _____ it would look nice. In _____, the appearance of her house _____ an obsession.

CHAPTER 18

VICTORY IN THE WATER

Prereading

Discuss these questions before reading the story.

1. What are you most afraid of? Closed-in places, like elevators? Sharks? Muggers? Disease? Something else?
2. What could you do to overcome your fear?

Reading Guide Questions

Think about these questions while you read. Be ready to answer them when you finish.

1. What is Olga afraid of? Why?
2. Does she overcome her fear? If so, how?

When Olga was five years old, her older brother, Mario, drowned at Mar del Plata. He was a good swimmer, but the ocean waves in that part of the coast of Argentina can be very strong. One very big wave came, and Mario disappeared. When this happened, Olga was playing on the beach with her mother. Suddenly her mother began to scream because she could not see Mario. Mario's body was never discovered.

After Mario's sad death in the water, Olga's mother and father wouldn't allow her to enter the water. They wanted to protect her. They did not want her to drown like Mario. For ten years, Olga and her parents did not go to any beach or river, not even for a picnic.

When Olga was fifteen years old, her mother and father decided to go to the beach. They thought it was all right to go to the beach, but they did not want Olga to go into the water. But after three hours in the hot sun, Olga was attracted to the cool water. She walked closer and closer to the water. Then, cautiously, she put one foot in the water. The water was so cold that it surprised her. She jerked her foot out because she was afraid. But then she realized that the water was not really bad, and she dipped her foot in it again. It was cool and pleasant, and she liked it.

All of a sudden, Olga's mother began to scream. Olga was standing in water that reached her waist. Her mother was so nervous and frightened that Olga ran out of the water and did not go back in all day.

When Olga was eighteen years old, her parents finally decided to let her go to the beach with a group from her high school. It was difficult for Olga's mother, but she finally agreed that this was the best thing for Olga. But she talked to the teacher who was responsible for the activity, and she asked the teacher to watch Olga diligently. She told the teacher that Olga did not know how to swim and said that Olga should not go into the water above her waist.

When the group arrived at the beach, the teacher told everyone to be very careful. Then she talked to Olga alone. She told her to be especially careful and to stay in shallow water.

But Olga liked the cool water on her skin. She liked it so much that she started toward the horizon. Soon she was in water almost up to her shoulders. She was happy and excited, not afraid. She continued slowly toward the horizon.

All at once, her foot plunged downward. She could not touch the ocean floor. She screamed, and then her head disappeared under the water. The teacher heard Olga scream and jumped in the water. She swam toward Olga. Olga's head had appeared and disappeared again. The teacher dove and pulled her up. When they surfaced, Olga was motionless. The teacher swam quickly to the beach. There she gave Olga emergency treatment because she was not breathing. At first, Olga did not respond. The teacher tried again. Then Olga vomited some water and began to breathe.

After this incident, Olga was terrified of the water and did not want to go to the beach. But now her parents believed that she was developing an abnormal fear. They decided that she should learn to swim so she would feel normal and happy like other girls her age.

One day Olga was reading a book when her boyfriend, José, called. He asked if she would like to go to the beach. At first, she did not want to go. But finally she decided to go to be with her boyfriend.

When they reached the ocean, Olga explained about her fear of the water. José was understanding and gentle with Olga. He told her that she could learn to swim gradually. At first she resisted. But José's love and affection made her feel safe.

At last José convinced Olga to try to float. They entered the water an inch at a time. Olga held tightly to José's hands. When they were in three feet of water, he showed her how to blow air bubbles. Olga tried it. After that, he showed her how to float. Then Olga tried. She was nervous, but she wanted to make José happy and she wanted to overcome her fear. For a minute she looked at him. She seemed to be absorbing confidence. Finally she lay flat in the water and blew bubbles. When she stood up, she was joyous.

It was easy to float! She was not afraid now. She had defeated her fear.

EXERCISES

Comprehension Questions

These questions are related to the reading guide questions that preceded the story. Answer them and be ready to support your answers when necessary.

1. What event caused Olga's parents to prohibit her from going into the ocean?
2. Who seems to be most strongly affected by this event, Olga or her parents?
3. How long did Olga's parents wait before deciding to go to the beach again?
4. What happens when they finally do go to the beach again?
5. What happens when Olga goes to the beach with her high school group? How does this affect her attitude toward the water?
6. How does she finally overcome her fear?

Questions for Further Discussion or Writing

Choose one question and discuss it in class or write a one-paragraph response. If you write a paragraph, you may wish to read it in class and discuss it.

1. Do you think Olga's parents did the best thing for Olga by waiting tens years to let her go to the beach again? Why or why not? Would you have acted differently? Explain.
2. Compare Olga's parents to Maritza's parents in "The Costly Decision." Are there similarities? Differences?
3. Have you ever overcome a fear? If so, how did you do it?

Optional Writing Exercise

If you do not like the title of this story, create a new one and explain in a short paragraph why you consider your title better.

Obtaining Meaning from Context

If you do not recognize a word or expression based on its appearance, you may be able to *guess* its meaning based on context. Try to guess the meaning of the *italicized* expression. If possible, make your guess in English.

1. She *jerked* her foot out because she was afraid.
2. But then she realized that the water was not really bad, and she *dipped* her foot in it again.
3. She told her to be especially careful and to stay in *shallow* water.
4. *All at once*, her foot *plunged* downward. She could not touch the ocean floor.
5. The teacher dove and pulled her up. When they *surfaced*, Olga was motionless.
6. They entered the water *an inch at a time*.
7. She was not afraid now. She had *defeated* her fear.

Cloze Exercise

Do this exercise in class unless otherwise instructed. You may work individually or in groups, but do not consult the original text for answers. When you finish, your teacher will have you check your answers. It is not necessary for your answers to be the same as those in the story, but they should be logical. When your answers differ from those in the story, discuss why they are or are not logical. *Note:* This exercise is not intended for use as a test or graded assignment.

When Olga was eighteen years _____, her parents finally decided to _____ her go to the beach _____ _____ a group from her high _____. It was difficult for Olga's _____, but she finally agreed that _____ _____ was the best thing for Olga. _____ she talked to the teacher _____ was responsible for the activity, _____ she asked the teacher to _____ Olga diligently. She told the _____ that Olga did not know _____ to swim and said that Olga _____ not go into water above _____ waist.

CHAPTER 19

THE HANDSOME UGLY BOY

Prereading

Discuss these questions before reading the story.

1. What do the words *handsome* and *ugly* mean? How can a person be handsome and ugly simultaneously?
2. Have you ever known someone who was like this? If so, describe your experience with this person.

Reading Guide Question

Think about this question while reading and be ready to answer it when you finish.

How was Hector both handsome and ugly?

It was Maria's first day at the university. The other students were throwing water balloons at her because she was a freshman. But there was one young man who was dressed nicely and acted differently. He was not a freshman, either. He was an upperclassman. He looked mature and sophisticated. His hair and clothing were neat and in good taste and his manner was friendly and dignified. He walked to where Maria was standing, defending herself against the onslaught of water balloons by holding her books in front of her face, and he took her by the arm. He guided her past the hooting crowd and took her to a more comfortable, private place. Then he introduced himself. His name was Hector. He said that he was a junior, a third-year student, in biology. He told her that he would like to get to know her better and he asked her if she would like to go to a movie with him on Saturday. Maria became nervous. Her parents had warned her against going out with strange men. She was a little frightened, but Hector seemed very nice. She thought for awhile, but then she said no. She said she did not know him well enough to go out with him yet. Hector smiled. He said that it was perfectly all right. He would ask her out again in the future.

During that week, Maria observed Hector talking with his friends and teachers. She asked people about him, and everyone said that Hector was a mature, responsible young man with a good reputation. When she asked his teachers, they said he was a good student and that his behavior in the classroom was exemplary.

When Friday came, Maria saw Hector in the cafeteria. He was eating lunch with a friend. Maria sat down nearby to observe him, and in a few minutes Hector's friend stood up from the table and left. Then Maria walked over to Hector's table. She sat down and they began to talk. When they left the cafeteria, they had decided to go out together on Saturday.

Saturday came, and Maria was happy, nervous, and excited. She imagined the future and what might happen if she and Hector liked each other a lot. She considered him handsome, intelligent, and polite, and she hoped that they would become closer.

Hector finally arrived, and with him he had brought a bouquet of flowers. He gave them to Maria and then introduced himself to her parents. In a few minutes, he had impressed Maria's parents. They considered him highly personable and thought he had a good future.

Hector took Maria to a movie, which they both enjoyed. After the movie, they got something to eat. Then he asked her to go dancing. It was late, but Maria did not want to disappoint him. He had been so nice that she felt obligated to say yes. They went dancing and enjoyed it very much; however, at eleven o'clock, she decided it was time to leave. She told Hector and he agreed, but when they got in the car he tried to seduce her. She resisted his advances and asked him to take her home, but he refused. He drove his car to a dark place and stopped. Maria was terrified. When he put his hand on her knee, she began to tremble. She felt like crying. She tried to scream, but Hector put his hand over her mouth.

Just then a police car appeared. Hector was so surprised that he was distracted. It was Maria's only opportunity. She jerked loose and ran from the car. The police saw her and came to her rescue. If they had arrived later, something terrible might have happened.

EXERCISES

Comprehension Questions

These questions are related to the reading guide question that preceded the story. When you answer, be prepared to support your answers where necessary with information from the story.

1. Under what circumstances did Maria meet Hector?
2. What impression did she have of him?

3. What did she do before going out with Hector?
4. What did other people say about him?
5. What kind of an impression did Hector make on Maria's parents?
6. Where do Maria and Hector go on their date?
7. Does Maria have a good time initially?
8. What happens to change things?
9. Who helps Maria?
10. Why is the story called "The Handsome Ugly Boy"?

Questions for Further Discussion or Writing

Choose one question and discuss it in class or write a paragraph in response. If you write a paragraph, you may wish to read and discuss it in class.

1. What can a girl do to avoid rape? Make a list and explain your ideas where necessary.
2. Do girls sometimes invite rape? Explain and, if possible, give examples.

Optional Writing Exercise

Describe a famous person who is simultaneously handsome and ugly. The person can be real or fictitious, living or dead. Work in groups and write your description in a few sentences. Do not mention the person's name so that other people in the class can guess his or her identity.

Obtaining Meaning from Context

If you do not recognize a word or expression based on its appearance, you may be able to *guess* its meaning based on context. Try to guess the meaning of the *italicized* expression. If possible, make your guess in English.

1. He was not a freshman, either. He was an *upperclassman*.
2. He walked to where Maria was standing, defending herself against the *onslaught* of water balloons by holding her books in front of her face, and he took her by the arm.

3. He guided her past the *hooting* crowd and took her to a more comfortable, private place.
4. He told her that he would like to *get to know* her better and he asked her if she would like to go to a movie with him on Saturday.
5. Her parents had warned her against *going out with* strange men.
6. She considered him handsome, intelligent, and *polite*, and she hoped that they would become closer.
7. It was late, but Maria did not want to *disappoint* him. He had been so nice that she felt obligated to say yes.
8. She told Hector and he agreed, but when they got in the car he tried to seduce her. She resisted his *advances* and asked him to take her home, but he refused.

Cloze Exercise

Do this exercise in class, unless otherwise instructed by your teacher. You may work in groups or individually, but do not consult the original text for answers. When you finish, your teacher will have you check your answers. It is not necessary for your answers to be the same as those in the story, but they should be logical. When your answers differ from those in the story, discuss why they are or are not logical. *Note*: This exercise is not intended as a test or graded assignment.

Hector took Maria to a _____, which they both enjoyed. After _____ movie, they got something to _____. Then he asked her to _____ dancing. It was late, but _____ did not want to disappoint _____. He had been so nice _____ she felt obligated to say _____. They went dancing and enjoyed _____ very much; however, at eleven _____, she decided it was time _____ leave. She told Hector and _____ agreed, but when they got _____ the car he tried to _____ her. She resisted his advances _____ asked him to take her _____, but he refused. He drove _____ car to a dark place

The Handsome Ugly Boy

_____ stopped. Maria was terrified. When _____ _____ put his hand on her _____, she began to tremble. She _____ like crying. She tried to _____ but Hector put his hand _____ her mouth.

CHAPTER 20

THE ABORTION

Prereading

Discuss the following questions before reading the story.

1. What is an abortion?
2. Why do people have abortions?

Reading Guide Questions

Think about these questions while you read and be ready to answer them when you finish.

1. Why does Maria consider having an abortion?
2. Does she have the abortion? Why or why not?

José was in a hurry. He walked rapidly toward the park. He hurried because Maria had called him on the telephone and told him to meet her in the park in fifteen minutes. She had something important to talk about. José was nervous because she had sounded scared and upset.

In the park, Maria was waiting for José. She knew that he would come soon. She was afraid and nervous because he would probably be unhappy about the news. Then he appeared. They kissed each other passionately and embraced. Then José looked into her eyes and asked her what she wanted to talk about. Maria became nervous. She looked at the ground at her feet. When she looked at José again, she was crying. When he asked her why she was crying, she said she was pregnant; she was going to have a baby.

Maria looked into José's eyes and asked him how he felt. José looked at a bird that was soaring in the blue sky. He thought about his own liberty, and tears came into his eyes. He told Maria that the baby was a big problem. He wanted to finish school and find a job before having a family. He loved her and he wanted to marry her. He was crying because having a baby now was inconvenient. If Maria had a baby now, José would be forced to quit school.

When José said these things, Maria cried. She believed that he did not want the baby. She fled from the park, crying. Confused about his feelings, José went home to think.

For a week, they did not see each other. Every time José called,

Maria said she wanted to be alone. She said she wanted to think. José said it was all right. He was thinking, too.

Maria was confused and unhappy. She felt divided between José and the baby. She wanted to make José happy, but she wanted the baby, too. The decision to have an abortion almost destroyed her. She confided her decision only to her diary. When she finished writing in her diary, she went out of the house.

The same day, José decided that the baby was more important than his career plans. He knew that Maria wanted the baby more than anything else. If the baby died, there would be no love.

José was relieved because he knew his decision was good. He went to Maria's house to talk to her. When he arrived, Maria was gone. José asked where she was, but her mother did not know. He thanked her and asked her to have Maria call him when she returned. Then he left.

During this time, Maria had taken the bus to a small barrio in the country. There she knew a lady who would perform the abortion.

Suddenly José had a terrible thought. He imagined that Maria had decided to get an abortion. At first he rejected this possibility. Then he began to believe it. He imagined Maria's suffering. He imagined her difficulty in making the decision. He imagined her sacrificing the baby for him. If this were true, José would never forgive himself. He turned around and ran toward Maria's house.

When he arrived, Maria's mother was surprised to see him. She asked why he had returned, and he told her the truth, including his fears. Maria's mother became nervous and started to cry. José tried to calm her down, but she cried for nearly an hour. Then she stopped suddenly and walked determinedly toward Maria's room. She opened a drawer and pulled out her daughter's diary. For a moment, she paused because she did not want to invade her daughter's privacy. But this was an emergency. Maybe there was something in the diary that would help them determine where Maria had gone. Maria's mother found the key and opened the diary. She turned to the last page and read it out loud. After that, there was nothing she and José could do but wait.

Several hours passed and Maria did not return. Her mother would cry from time to time, and José was pacing the floor. All at once, the door opened and Maria walked in. Her mother and boyfriend both looked at her. Maria saw that her mother had been crying and imagined the reason. She told José and her mother the truth.

After that, Maria continued to live with her mother. José began college. They did not get married. They did not see each other often because José stayed in another town while he was studying.

One day, after an exam, José decided to call Maria. They talked for an hour on the telephone. Afterward, José felt content. He went back to his studies feeling good. The baby was fine. Maria was fine. When José graduated, he and Maria would be married.

EXERCISES

Comprehension Questions

These questions are related to the reading guide questions that preceded the story. When you answer them, be ready to support your answers with information from the story where necessary.

1. What news does Maria give José in the park?
2. How does he react and why?
3. How does José really feel about Maria? How do you know?
4. What did Maria decide to do? Why?
5. How did José and Maria's mother discover her plans?
6. Did Maria have the abortion?
7. Was the story's ending happy or unhappy? Explain.

Questions for Further Discussion or Writing

Choose one question and discuss it in class or write a brief paragraph in response. If you write a paragraph, you may wish to read and discuss it in class.

1. How do you feel about abortion and why?
2. If you are against abortion, try to think of circumstances that might justify an abortion and describe them.

Optional Writing Exercise

Consider the last three paragraphs, the ending of the story. Rewrite the ending and in doing so consider the following questions: Does Maria have the abortion? Do she and José get married? Does he continue his studies? Is the ending a happy one?

Obtaining Meaning from Context

If you do not recognize a word or expression based on its appearance, you may be able to *guess* its meaning based on context. Try to guess the meaning of the *italicized* expression. If possible, make your guess in English.

1. José looked at a bird that was *soaring* in the blue sky.
2. If Maria had a baby now, José would be forced to *quit* school.
3. She *fled* from the park, crying.
4. He imagined her sacrificing the baby for him. If this were true, José would never *forgive* himself.
5. Her mother would cry *from time to time*, and José was pacing the floor.

Cloze Exercise

Do this exercise in class unless otherwise instructed. You may work in groups or individually, but do not consult the original text for answers. When you finish, your teacher will have you check your answers. It is not necessary for your answers to be the same as those in the story, but they should be logical. When your answers differ from those in the story, discuss why they are or are not logical. *Note*: This exercise is not intended as a test or graded assignment.

Suddenly José had a terrible _____. He imagined that Maria had _____ to get an abortion. At _____ he rejected this possibility. Then _____ began to believe it. He _____ Maria's suffering. He imagined her _____ in making the decision. He _____ her sacrificing the baby for _____. If this were true, José _____ never forgive himself. He turned _____ _____ and ran toward Maria's house.

CHAPTER 21

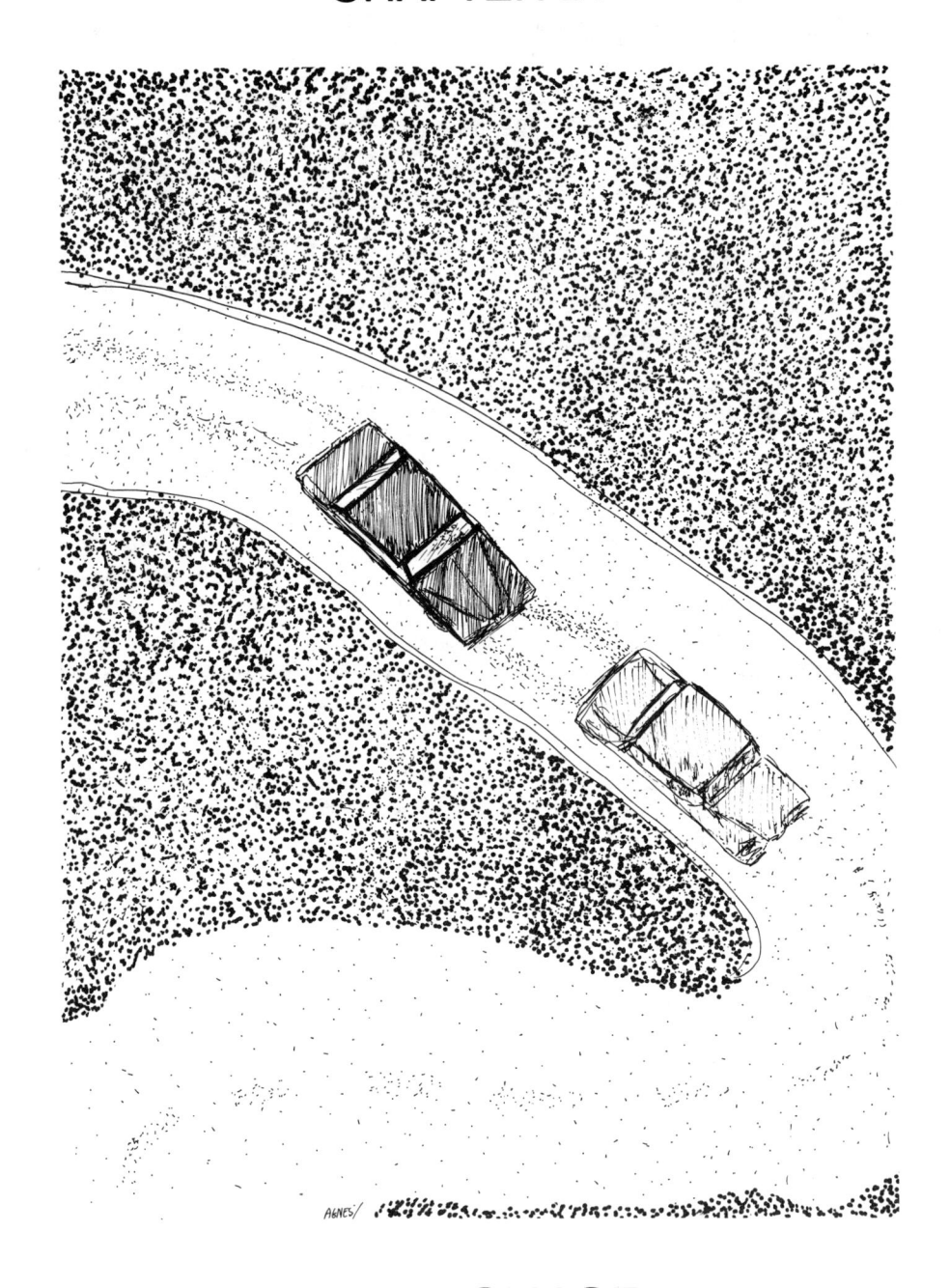

THE CHASE
(based on a true incident)

Prereading

Discuss these questions before reading the story.

Have you ever been chased by someone without knowing why the person was chasing you? If so, how did you feel? If not, how do you imagine you would feel?

Reading Guide Questions

Think about these questions while reading and be prepared to answer them when you finish.

1. Who is chasing the two girls?
2. What is your opinion of his behavior?

My younger sister and I were alone on the road between two towns. It was eleven o'clock at night, and there were practically no cars on the road. Our old car putted along at forty miles per hour. I drove slowly because of the dark and curvy road. Suddenly a car came around the curve behind us, going very fast. The girl driving the car passed us carelessly and disappeared in the distance. Then, in my rear-view mirror, the headlights of another car became visible. This car was also moving with great speed, so I decided to slow down to let the driver pass. But when I slowed down, he slowed down too. So I went faster. But he went faster too. Then we reached a straight portion of road and the man pulled alongside of us and started shouting vulgar suggestions. I remembered my husband's comment that women should never drive alone at night, and I became more scared.

    The road got curvy again and the man fell in behind us. He tailgated us constantly, and this made us nervous because we thought there would be a collision.

    Suddenly he turned on a police siren. I decided not to stop because I thought he wasn't really a policeman. Besides, his behavior was not normal. All this time, my sister and I could not speak because we were so frightened. After a few minutes, the man increased his speed and started to pass us with his siren still on. When he was beside us he turned on the inside light and held up a police badge. Then he signalled for us to pull over. But I continued to drive as fast as I could. I could not see his insignia well at night, and I did not trust him.

But he had not finished with us yet. When we refused to stop, he began banging our car with his. Finally he hit us so hard that we went off the road. When we were trying to get back on, he pulled his car in front of us and stopped in our path. Then we had to stop.

I prayed to God that he would not hurt us. He was a big man. I saw this as he stepped out of the car. He walked slowly toward us. When he reached our car window and bent over, I could not breathe because I was too terrified.

When he asked for my license, I nodded and handed it to him. Then he asked why I hadn't stopped and I whispered that I was scared. He laughed a strange laugh and said I shouldn't have been scared. He said that he was there to protect us. Then he laughed again and told me one of my car's tail lights was out. After that, he gave us a ticket and left. Then we began to breathe again. The chase was over.

EXERCISES

Comprehension Questions

These questions are related to the reading guide questions that preceded the story. When you answer, be prepared to support your answers where necessary with information from the story.

1. Describe the chase.
2. How did the two girls feel?
3. How did they discover that the man was chasing them?
4. Who was the man?
5. How did he stop them?
6. How did he behave?

Questions for Further Discussion or Writing

Choose one question and discuss it in class or write a brief paragraph in response. If you write a paragraph, you may wish to read and discuss it in class.

1. If you were in this situation, how would you react? What would you do?

2. Have you ever had an experience with someone who was mentally disturbed? If so, describe your experience.

Optional Writing Exercise

Give this story a new title. In a short paragraph, explain why your title is better than the original.

Obtaining Meaning from Context

If you do not recognize a word or expression based on its appearance, you may be able to *guess* its meaning based on context. Try to guess the meaning of the *italicized* expression. If possible, make your guess in English.

1. Our old car *putted along* at forty miles per hour.
2. Then, in my *rear-view mirror*, the headlights of another car became visible.
3. He *tailgated* us constantly, and this made us nervous because we thought there would be a collision.
4. ... he turned on the inside light and held up a police badge. Then he signalled for us to *pull over*.
5. When he asked for my license, I nodded and *handed* it to him.

Cloze Exercise

Do this exercise in class, unless otherwise instructed. You may work individually or in groups, but do not consult the original text for answers. When you finish, your teacher will have you check your answers. It is not necessary for your answers to be the same as those in the story, but they should be logical. When your answers differ from those in the story, discuss why they are or are not logical. *Note*: This exercise is not intended as a test or graded assignment.

    Suddenly he turned on a _____ siren. I decided not to _____ because I thought he wasn't _____ a policemen. Besides, his behavior _____ not normal. All

118   The Chase

this time, _____ sister and I could not _____ because we were so frightened. _____ a few minutes, the man _____ his speed and started to _____ us with his siren still _____. When he was beside us, _____ turned on the inside light _____ held up a police badge. _____ he signalled for us to _____ over. But I continued to _____ as fast as I could. _____ could not see his insignia _____ at night, and I did _____ trust him.

CHAPTER 22

THE OUTSIDER

Prereading

Discuss the following questions before reading the story.

1. What is an outsider?
2. What are some reasons why a person is considered an outsider?
3. Can you think of an example of a person you know who was or is treated as an outsider?

Reading Guide Questions

Think about these questions while you read and be prepared to answer them after you finish.

1. Why is Jorge an outsider?
2. Does he remain an outsider?

Jorge was a young boy. His face was long, his skin was dark, his hair was straight, and his body was thin. He lived in Oaxaca. In Oaxaca, Jorge's family cultivated the soil and raised corn and beans. Most people in Oaxaca spoke Mixteco or Zapoteco. Jorge spoke Zapoteco. He knew some Spanish, but he was not very fluent.

When Jorge was eight years old, his parents decided to move to Mexico City to look for better employment. In Mexico City, his father found employment loading and unloading fruit trucks. His mother found work in the home of a family with money. Jorge and his family lived in the poverty belt that exists on the outskirts of Mexico City.

Soon Jorge was enrolled in an elementary school. He would be in the first grade because he was not fluent in Spanish. Finally, the first day of class came. When he entered the first-grade room, he was greeted by the laughter of the other children. Some of them were pointing at him and whispering to other students. One boy put his hands to his face and pulled the skin downward to imitate Jorge's long face and the sad expression in his eyes. Another boy commented audibly about his clothing. Jorge's pants were very old and discolored and he wore huaraches on his feet. All this identified Jorge as a poor Indian boy. In contrast, the other children seemed to come from families of a relatively high economic status. They had new clothing and their faces were round and plump.

Jorge felt embarrassed. His skin felt hot, but he was too humble to retaliate. The teacher finally ordered the other children to be quiet, and she gave them a look of disapproval. However, they continued to whisper comments about Jorge.

Jorge took a seat in the back of the room and was very quiet. Whenever the teacher called him, he lowered his head because he did not want the others to laugh at the way he spoke.

As time passed, the other children became bored with ridiculing Jorge, but they still did not accept him. Jorge was very quiet and alone.

One day the teacher took the children on a field trip to the National Museum of Anthropology. All the students were excited, except Jorge. He was afraid. The museum was full of many interesting things, especially works created by indigenous peoples. The teacher stopped the group in front of several exhibitons to explain their importance. Finally, they stopped in front of a statue called "Esplendido excribo zapoteca." The teacher explained to the class that this wonderful piece of art had been created by a Zapoteco Indian. When she said this, Jorge's eyes brightened with recognition. Then the teacher reminded the class that Jorge, too, was Zapoteco. She was demonstrating to the other students that Jorge's people were culturally important. She explained that the statue of the scribe had been discovered in Jorge's state, Oaxaca, in Culiapán. Oaxaca, she told them, was important culturally. She mentioned Monte Albán, the excellence of the work of the native artisans, and other things.

When the tour of the museum had finished, the children returned to the school. On the way, they began to ask Jorge questions about Oaxaca and the Zapoteco Indians. Jorge was surprised and happy because he discovered that he had something interesting to offer the other children. The other children became so interested in the theme that the teacher decided to ask Jorge to talk in class about Oaxaca and Zapoteco customs. Suddenly Jorge was not an outsider. He felt proud, happy, and accepted.

EXERCISES

Comprehension Questions

These questions are related to the reading guide questions that preceded the story. Answer these questions and be prepared to justify your answers based on information from the story.

1. Describe Jorge.
2. Describe his family.
3. Where does his family move and why?
4. How do the other children initially react to Jorge? Be specific.
5. Why do they react that way?
6. How does the teacher help Jorge?
7. What change occurs in the attitude of the other children toward Jorge and why?

Questions for Further Discussion or Writing

Choose one question and discuss it in class or write a brief paragraph in response. If you write a paragraph, you may wish to read and discuss it in class.

1. Give examples of famous outsiders or outsiders you know personally. Why are (were) these people outsiders? If they are no longer outsiders, how or why did they become accepted?
2. Suppose you moved to another country and found that people treated you as an outsider. How would you feel and what would you do? Would you want to remain an outsider? Would you wait passively and hope for acceptance? Would you work actively to be accepted? If so, how would you go about achieving acceptance?

Optional Writing Exercise

Give the story a new title and write a brief paragraph explaining why you prefer the new title to the original.

Obtaining Meaning from Context

If you do not recognize a word or expression based on its appearance, you may be able to *guess* its meaning based on context. Try to guess the meaning of the *italicized* expression. If possible, make your guess in English.

1. In Mexico City, his father found employment *loading* and *unloading* fruit trucks.

2. Jorge and his family lived in the poverty belt that exists on the *outskirts* of Mexico City.
3. Soon Jorge was *enrolled* in an elementary school.
4. Some of them were pointing at him and *whispering* to other students.
5. They had new clothing and their faces were round and *plump*.
6. Jorge felt *embarrassed*.
7. His skin felt hot, but he was too *humble* to retaliate.

Cloze Exercise

Do this exercise in class, unless otherwise instructed. You may work in groups or individually, but do not consult the original text for answers. When you finish, your teacher will have you check your answers. It is not necessary for your answers to be the same as those in the story, but they should be logical. When your answers differ from those in the story, discuss why they are or are not logical. *Note*: This exercise is not intended as a test or graded assignment.

Jorge was a young boy. _____ face was long, his skin _____ dark, his hair was straight, _____ his body was thin. He _____ in Oaxaca. In Oaxaca, Jorge's _____ cultivated the soil and raised _____ and beans. Most people in _____ spoke Mixteco or Zapoteco. Jorge _____ Zapoteco. He knew some Spanish, _____ he was not very fluent.

CHAPTER 23

THE BLIND BASKETBALL PLAYER

Prereading

Discuss the following questions before reading the story.

1. What does the word *handicap* mean? What are some handicaps?
2. Do you know anyone with a handicap? If so, how has this person adapted to his handicap?

Reading Guide Questions

Think about these questions while you read and be prepared to answer them after you finish.

1. Did Raul adapt to his handicap?
2. How did different people motivate or influence him?

This is the phenomenal story of a blind basketball player. It is like a miracle, but he learned to sense everything around him.

Raul Ferre was five years old when he lost the vision in both eyes. Raul's father was a brilliant chemist. He did some experiments in one of the rooms of their house. He called this room his laboratory. One day he left the laboratory open. Raul entered the laboratory because he was curious. He tried to reach an object on a tall shelf, but the object was very heavy. Suddenly it toppled over and knocked him unconscious. When he regained consciousness, he could not see. His vision never returned.

For a long time, Raul was depressed. He could not adjust to his new situation. It was a terrible handicap to be blind. He could not see anything, and so he believed he could not do anything. He was afraid to walk from his bedroom to the kitchen.

Then one day Raul's father talked with him. He talked about Raul's handicap. He encouraged Raul to try to do things. This made Raul decide to try to adjust to reality.

First he tried to walk to the kitchen. It wasn't easy. He wanted to walk fast and straight like a normal boy. This was not possible. The first time he attempted it, he walked into a chair and fell to the floor. He decided it was necessary to use his hands. He put his hands in front of him and walked slowly toward the door of the bedroom. When he reached the door, his fingers bumped the wood. This made him stop. He moved his hand and tried to discover the doorknob. He found it and opened the door. This was his first triumph.

After weeks of practicing, Raul found that he could walk to the bedroom door and open it very quickly and easily. Then he began to try other things. He tried to find his clothes inside his dresser and closet. He tried to distinguish different socks, shoes, shirts, and pants. But this was very difficult. How could he recognize the difference between a red shirt and a green shirt if he could not see? Raul became angry and threw all his clothes on the floor in a heap. Then he jumped on them and screamed in a loud, pathetic voice.

Then Raul's father came to him and talked with him again. Raul's father was a very intelligent, analytical man, and he was also very patient with Raul. He took him to the bed and sat him there. Then he brought him a shirt. He put it in Raul's hands and asked him to feel it carefully all over. Raul felt every part of the shirt, but he could not tell which shirt it was. Then Raul's father asked Raul if he had noticed anything special about this shirt. Raul said no. His father told him to feel the pocket. Raul felt the pocket and then smiled. The pocket had a crocodile. It was an old shirt. He remembered that it was red. They took another shirt. Raul felt it carefully. He noticed that it had a very smooth texture. That must be one of his white shirts for Sunday school and church. After several more efforts, Raul discovered that it was fun to guess the identity of different articles of clothing. It was easy for him.

The years passed. Raul entered high school at Colegio Marham in Lima. He had learned to read by using special books. The books had symbols that he could read by touching them with his fingers. Raul had no problems with his school subjects because all of his books were in Braille and he could read them all with his fingers. His mind was very agile, and he had learned to imagine things that he could not see. As a result, he was a brilliant student. He did not have to study very much. Soon he became bored because he had nothing to do with his time.

One day he was outside on the basketball court, waiting for physical education class to begin, when somebody hit his chest with a basketball. The ball bounced off his chest and onto the court. Raul was surprised. Then he heard a voice asking him if he wanted to play basketball. He recognized the voice of José Seriedeuno. José was Raul's worst enemy. Raul hated him because he was always laughing at people and making fun of them. Raul had never played basketball before. In fact, he only had a vague idea of what a basketball was. He only knew that it was a big ball that bounced. Now he was angry. He wanted to show

José—to beat José at basketball. He accepted José's ironic invitation to play. But Raul did not know that it was impossible to play basketball without vision.

The game began. Raul asked José how to play. José explained, and then they started playing. Raul tried to dribble the ball against the floor, but José knocked it away with his hand. He stole the ball from Raul and made one basket after another. Soon, José had thirty-two points and Raul had zero. The game was over. José laughed and went away. Raul stood alone in the middle of the court.

In the weeks that followed, Raul visited the basketball court every day for an hour or two. He was accompanied by his best friend, Marcelo. Marcelo described the court to Raul. He told him the height of the basketball net. He told him the dimensions of the court. He told him where the free-throw line was located. He even took Raul to different spots on the court. Slowly Raul began to see the court in his mind. But he still did not know very much about playing the game.

On the weekend, Raul's father talked to him. He could see that Raul had a problem; it was reflected in his face. He asked Raul what the problem was, and the boy explained. After that, Mr. Ferre took Raul to the park. Mr. Ferre did not know how to play basketball very well, but there were some boys playing in the park. He asked them if they would teach Raul. They said yes and began to involve Raul in the game. When they shot the ball, Raul put his hands on their chests so he could imagine how they jumped. He asked them many questions, and he asked them to put his hands in the correct position for shooting the ball. For many weekends, this process continued. Eventually Raul learned the right way to hold the ball, the right way to shoot the ball, the right way to pass the ball, and the right way to dribble the ball. But there was still one big problem: Raul had never scored points. That is, he had never put the basketball through the basket. Every time he tried, he missed by two or three feet. He just could not imagine the position of the basket. Then one day Raul's father had an idea.

The next weekend, Raul's father surprised Raul with a gift. He told him that the gift would help him play basketball better. Raul did not understand. The gift was a Christmas decoration: a long string of bells that made a musical sound when you moved them. How could this help Raul to play basketball better? Mr. Ferre took Raul to the park to demonstrate how the bells worked.

At the park, they found the boys who usually helped Raul. Mr. Ferre gave the decoration to one of the boys and whispered something to him. The boy smiled and reacted quietly. When he had finished, the boys began to shoot the ball. Suddenly, Raul heard the Christmas bells making musical sounds. Then he understood! Every time the ball touched the basket, the bells would sound. This would help him to imagine the position of the basket. Now Raul was excited. He took the ball and threw it in the direction of the sound. The ball hit the backboard near the basket and the bells sounded. Raul was happy. He asked if he had scored two points. His father explained that he had come close. Raul tried very hard, again and again, but he only came close. When the day was finished, he was a little sad, but the music of the bells gave him hope.

Raul practiced with the Christmas bells every weekend for more than three months. Then one day he was playing with his friends and something incredible happened. Raul was in the middle of a jump shot. He moved up through the air. Suddenly, as he positioned the ball to take the shot, he saw the basket in his mind. In fact, he saw everything in his mind at that moment. He saw the red belt-like decoration that was hanging from the bottom of the backboard. He could see the eight bells, all silver-colored. He knew in some strange way where each of his friends was standing at that moment. He scored! There was total silence. Then everyone was cheering and congratulating him. He had scored his first basket.

The weeks passed, and Raul continued to practice. Now he would make a basket ten percent of the time. But this did not make him happy. He wanted to beat José Seríedeuno. He continued to practice at the school basketball court with Marcelo. Marcelo did not have to tell him when he scored a basket; Raul had learned to listen for the sound of the ball passing through the net. In addition, there was a spot on the court near the free-throw line that Raul recognized when his feet touched it. This helped his shooting percentage to improve. One day Marcelo and Raul were playing. Marcelo was not playing very aggressively because he wanted Raul to win. Then Raul heard a familiar voice—a voice that he hated. Of course, it was José. He was laughing and saying that Marcelo was not trying. This made Raul so angry that he challenged José to play. José accepted.

The game began badly for Raul. José quickly made fourteen points, and Raul had zero. José began to laugh because Raul was losing. Raul's face turned red. He began to play more rapidly, and suddenly everything came together. Raul's increased momentum produced a change. His feet became intimate friends with the floor, his hands became part of the basketball, his body was in unity with the entire basketball court. In five minutes, the score was tied at fourteen. José was silent. Raul was happy inside. Then the momentum shifted again, this time in favor of José, and he won the game thirty-two to eighteen.

Raul felt disappointed. Then something happened that surprised him: José lifted Raul into the air. He was recognizing Raul's heroic effort. Raul had lost the basketball game, but he had won a friend.

EXERCISES

Comprehension Questions

These questions are related to the reading guide questions that preceded the story. Answer them and be prepared to justify your answers based on information from the story.

1. How did Raul lose his vision?
2. What was Raul's father's occupation?
3. What was Raul's first triumph?
4. How did Raul identify his clothes?
5. Was Raul a good student, an average student, or a poor student?
6. Why did he become interested in playing basketball?
7. How did Marcelo help him?
8. How did his father and the boys in the park help him?
9. What helped Raul to improve his accuracy? (*Hint*: It was his father's idea.)
10. What happened in the final game between Raul and José?

Questions for Further Discussion or Writing

Choose one question and discuss it in class or write a brief paragraph in response. If you write a paragraph, you may wish to read and discuss it in class.

1. Did Raul's father and José both motivate him? Explain.
2. Do you believe this story is possible? Why or why not?
3. How do you imagine the life of a blind person to be? What problems would there be?

4. What does this story say about the potential of people with handicaps? Do you know of any real-life examples that corroborate this view?

Optional Writing Exercise

Rewrite the story's ending (the last paragraph). In doing so, consider these questions: Who wins the game? What happens in the game to make it an important event in the story?

Obtaining Meaning from Context

If you do not recognize a word or expression based on its appearance, you may be able to *guess* its meaning based on context. Try to guess the meaning of the *italicized* expression. If possible, make your guess in English.

1. He tried to reach an object on a tall shelf, but the object was very heavy. Suddenly it *toppled over* and knocked him unconscious.
2. When he reached the door, his fingers *bumped* the wood.
3. He tried to find his clothes inside his dresser and *closet*.
4. Raul hated him because he was always laughing at people and *making fun of* them.
5. Raul tried to *dribble* the ball against the floor. . . .
6. The ball hit the backboard near the basket and the *bells* sounded.
7. He wanted to *beat* José Seriedeuno.

Cloze Exercise

Do this exercise in class, unless otherwise instructed. You may work individually or in groups, but do not consult the original text for answers. When you finish, your teacher will have you check your answers. It is not necessary for your answers to be the same as those in the story, but they should be logical. When your answers differ from those in the story, discuss why they are or are not logical. *Note*: This exercise is not intended as a test or graded assignment.

The years passed. Raul entered _____ school at Colegio Marham in Lima. _____ had learned to read by _____ special books. The books had _____ that he could read by _____ them with his fingers. Raul _____ no problems with his school _____ because all of his _____ were in Braille and he could read _____ all with his fingers. His _____ was very agile, and he _____ learned to imagine things that _____ could not see. As a _____, he was a brilliant student. _____ did not have to study _____ much. Soon he became bored _____ he had nothing to do _____ his time.